DORDT INFORMATION SERVICES
P9-DNX-480

THE EVOLUTION OF CAPITALISM

THE EVOLUTION
OF CAPITALISM

THE FREEDOM OF THE SEAS

OR

THE RIGHT WHICH BELONGS TO THE DUTCH TO TAKE PART IN THE EAST INDIAN TRADE

HUGO GROTIUS

ARNO PRESS
A NEW YORK TIMES COMPANY
New York • 1972

Reprint Edition 1972 by Arno Press Inc.

Reprinted from a copy in
The Wesleyan University Library

The Evolution of Capitalism
ISBN for complete set: 0-405-04110-1
See last pages of this volume for titles.

Manufactured in the United States of America

- - - - - - - - - - - - -

Library of Congress Cataloging in Publication Data

Grotius, Hugo, 1583-1645.
The freedom of the seas.

(The Evolution of capitalism)
Latin text of Mare liberum with English translation.
Latin and English on opposite pages, numbered in duplicate.
1. Maritime law. 2. Freedom of the seas.
I. Title. II. Series.
JX4423.G8 1972 341'.44 71-38252
ISBN 0-405-04123-3

HVGONIS GROTII

MARE LIBERVM

SIVE

DE IVRE QVOD BATAVIS

COMPETIT

AD INDICANA COMMERCIA,

DISSERTATIO

1608

Carnegie Endowment for International Peace
DIVISION OF INTERNATIONAL LAW

THE FREEDOM OF THE SEAS

OR

THE RIGHT WHICH BELONGS TO THE DUTCH TO TAKE PART IN THE EAST INDIAN TRADE

A DISSERTATION BY
HUGO GROTIUS

TRANSLATED WITH A REVISION OF THE LATIN TEXT OF 1633
BY
RALPH VAN DEMAN MAGOFFIN, PH.D.
Associate Professor of Greek and Roman History
The Johns Hopkins University

EDITED WITH AN INTRODUCTORY NOTE
BY
JAMES BROWN SCOTT
DIRECTOR

NEW YORK
OXFORD UNIVERSITY PRESS
AMERICAN BRANCH: 35 WEST 32ND STREET
LONDON, TORONTO, MELBOURNE, AND BOMBAY
HUMPHREY MILFORD
1916

THE QUINN & BODEN CO. PRESS
RAHWAY, N. J.

INTRODUCTORY NOTE

Since the month of August, 1914, the expression "Freedom of the Seas" has been on the lips alike of belligerent and neutral, and it seems as advisable as it is timely to issue—for the first time in English—the famous Latin tractate of Grotius proclaiming, explaining, and in no small measure making the "freedom of the seas." [1]

The title of the little book, first published, anonymously, in November, 1608, explains the reason for its composition: "The Freedom of the Seas, or the Right which belongs to the Dutch to take part in the East Indian trade." It was an open secret that it was written by the young Dutch scholar and lawyer, Hugo Grotius. It was a secret and remained a secret until 1868 that the *Mare Liberum* was none other than Chapter XII of the treatise *De Jure Praedae,* written by Grotius in the winter of 1604-5, which first came to light in 1864 and was given to the world four years later.[2]

The publication of the treatise on the law of prize is important as showing that the author of the *Mare Liberum* was already an accomplished international lawyer, and it

[1] For the freedom of the seas and the relation of Grotius to the doctrine, see Ernest Nys's *Les Origines du Droit International* (1894), pp. 379-387, and the same author's *Etudes de Droit International et de Droit Politique,* 2e série (1901), *Une Bataille de Livres,* pp. 260-272. For an account in English see Walker's *History of the Law of Nations,* Vol. I (1899), pp. 278-283.

For an interesting sketch of the illustrious author of the *Mare Liberum,* see Motley's *The Life and Death of John of Barneveld,* Vol. II, Chap. XXII; for an analysis of Grotius' views on the law of nations, see Hallam's *Introduction to the Literature of Europe* (4th edition), Vol. II, Part III, Chap. IV, Sec. III; for an account of Grotius as a humanist, see Sandys' *History of Classical Scholarship* (1908), Vol. II, pp. 315-319.

[2] *Hugonis Grotii De Jure Praedae,* edited, with an introduction, by H. G. Hamaker, and published at The Hague in 1868 by Martinus Nijhoff.

proves beyond peradventure that the masterpiece of 1625 on the "Law of War and Peace" was not a hurried production, but the culmination of study and reflection extending over twenty years and more. More important still is the fact that neither the law of prize nor the *Mare Liberum* was a philosophic exercise, for it appears that Grotius had been retained by the Dutch East India Company to justify the capture by one of its ships of a Portuguese galleon in the straits of Malacca in the year 1602; that the treatise on the law of prize, of which the *Mare Liberum* is a chapter, was in the nature of a brief; and that the first systematic treatise on the law of nations—The Law of War and Peace—was not merely a philosophical disquisition, but that it was the direct outgrowth of an actual case and of professional employment.[1]

[1] In support of the view that Grotius appeared as counsel in cases arising out of captures made by vessels in the service of the Dutch East India Company, and that the treatise, *De Jure Praedae,* is a legal brief, see R. Fruin's *Een Onuitgegeven Werk van Hugo De Groot* in *Verspreide Geschriften,* Vol. III, pp. 367-445. The following passages are quoted from this remarkable essay:

"While busy with the sale of the goods [of the captured merchantman *Catherine,* which had been unloaded in the Amsterdam arsenal], the process of adjudicating the booty before the admiralty court was conducted in the usual forms. Claimants: Advocate General of Holland, the Board of eight Aldermen, and Admiral Heemskerck; . . . on Thursday, September 9, 1604, final sentence was rendered, and 'the merchantman together with the goods taken from it were declared forfeited and confiscated'" (pp. 389-390).

"Hulsius in some measure replaces what the fire at the Marine Arsenal has robbed us of; among other records he has preserved for us in his *Achte Schiffart* the sentence pronounced in this matter by the admiralty, and of which we have knowledge from no other sources. From it we learn the grounds upon which the claimants demanded the adjudication of the booty. These grounds are the same twelve which De Groot discusses in his book. . . . This concordance can be explained on the ground that De Groot must have had acquaintance with the sentence; but he was not a man merely to repeat what others had before him witnessed. I should be inclined to feel that in the process he had served as counsel for the Company, and that he himself was one of the authors of the written claim upon which the sentence was based. It would not then be surprising if in his book he should develop at greater length and throw light upon what had already been set forth in the claim" (pp. 390-391).

"I cannot state definitely that Hugo De Groot was persuaded by the Directors to write such an argument; I have been unable to discover any evidence to

The Spaniards, as is well known, then claimed the Pacific Ocean and the Gulf of Mexico, and Portugal claimed, in like manner, the Atlantic south of Morocco and the Indian Ocean, and both nations, at this time under a common sovereign, claimed and sought to exercise the right of excluding all foreigners from navigating or entering these waters. The Dutch, then at war with Spain, although not technically at war with Portugal, established themselves in 1598 in the island of Mauritius. Shortly thereafter they made settlements in Java and in the Moluccas. In 1602 the Dutch East India Company was formed, and, as it attempted to trade with the East Indies, its vessels came into competition with those of the Portuguese engaged in the Eastern trade, which sought to exclude them from the Indian waters. One Heemskerck, a captain in the employ of the Company, took a large Portuguese galleon in the Straits of Malacca. To trade with the East Indies was one thing, to capture Portuguese vessels was quite another thing. Therefore, some members of the Company refused their parts of the prize; others sold their shares in the company, and still others thought of establishing a new company in France, under the protection of King Henry IV, which should trade in peace and abstain from all warlike action. The matter was therefore one of no little importance, and it appears that Grotius was consulted and wrote his treatise on the law of prize, which is in the nature of a brief and is, at any rate, a lawyer's argument.[1]

that end. That he was in close relations with the Company, he himself says in a letter of later date, addressed to his brother. Nor can there be any doubt that in writing his work he made use of the archives of the United Company and of its predecessor. If the supposition, which I have elsewhere ventured to make is correct, that is to say, that in the conduct of the case he appeared as advocate for the Company, it would then appear most probable that, after consultation with the directors, he set about writing his book, which was to be a second plea in their behalf" (p. 403).

[1] For the account which Grotius himself gives of the incident, see his *Annales et Historiae de Rebus Belgicis ab Obitu Philippi Regis usque ad Inducias Anni* 1609, written in 1612, but first published in 1658, Book 1, p. 429.

In 1608 Spain and Holland began negotiations which, on April 9, 1609, resulted in the truce of Antwerp for the period of 12 years, and, in the course of the negotiations, Spain tried to secure from the United Provinces a renunciation of their right to trade in the East and West Indies. The Dutch East India Company thereupon, it would appear, requested Grotius to publish that part of his brief dealing with the freedom of the seas. This was done under the title of *Mare Liberum,* with such changes as were necessary to enable it to stand alone.

It will be observed that the *Mare Liberum* was written to refute the unjustified claims of Spain and Portugal to the high seas and to exclude foreigners therefrom. The claims of England, less extensive but not less unjustifiable, were not mentioned, and yet, if the arguments of Grotius were sound, the English claims to the high seas to the south and east of England, as well as to undefined regions to the north and west, would likewise fall to the ground. Therefore the distinguished English lawyer, scholar, and publicist, John Selden by name, bestirred himself in behalf of his country and wrote his *Mare Clausum* in 1617 or 1618, although it was not published until 1635, to refute the little tractate, *Mare Liberum.*[1] In the dedication to King Charles I,

For a fuller account of the circumstances under which the treatise on the law of prize was written, see Hamaker's edition of the *De Jure Praedae,* pp. vii-viii. The distinguished historian and scholar, Robert J. Fruin, after an exhaustive examination of the evidence, informed Hamaker that Grotius was retained by the Company to prepare the commentary on the law of prize. The English translation of Hamaker's exact statement reads as follows: "Fruin is of the opinion that he [Grotius] undertook this work at the instance of the Company, and that he appeared in it as their spokesman."

For an analysis of the commentary *De Jure Praedae* and the circumstances under which it was written, see Jules Basdevant's study on Grotius, pp. 131-137, 155-179, in Pillet's *Les Fondateurs du Droit International* (1904).

[1] Selden's *Mare Clausum* was not the only defense of England, nor was the *Mare Liberum* the only lance which Grotius broke for the freedom of the seas. In 1613 William Welwod, professor of Civil Law at the University of Aberdeen, published a little book entitled *An Abridgement of all the Sea-Lawes,* in which he maintained the English side of the question, of which Title XXVII, pp. 61-

Selden said: "There are among foreign writers, who rashly attribute your Majesty's more southern and eastern sea to their princes. Nor are there a few, who following chiefly some of the ancient Caesarian lawyers, endeavor to affirm, or beyond reason too easily admit, that all seas are common to the universality of mankind." The thesis of Selden was twofold: first, "that the sea, by the law of nature or nations, is not common to all men, but capable of private dominion or property as well as the land"; second, "that the King of Great Britain is lord of the sea flowing about, as an inseparable and perpetual appendant of the British Empire."

In this battle of books, to use the happy expression of Professor Nys, the Dutch Scholar has had the better of his English antagonist. If it cannot be said that Grotius wears his learning "lightly like a flower", the treatise of Selden is, in comparison, over-freighted with it; the *Mare Liberum* is still an open book, the *Mare Clausum* is indeed a closed one, and as flotsam or jetsam on troubled waters, Chapter XII of the Law of Prize rides the waves, whereas its rival, heavy and water-logged, has gone under.

In the leading case of The Louis (2 Dodson 210), decided in 1817, some two hundred years after Selden's book was written, Sir William Scott, later Lord Stowell and one of Selden's most distinguished countrymen, said, in rejecting the claim of his country to the exercise of jurisdiction beyond a marine league from the British shore:

72, deals with the community and property of the seas. Two years later Welwod published a second work, this time in Latin, entitled *De Dominio Maris Juribusque ad Dominium praecipue Spectantibus Assertia Brevis ac Methodica.*

Grotius prepared, but did not publish, a reply to Welwod's first attack, entitled *Defensio Capitis Quinti Maris Liberi Oppugnati a Gulielmo Welwodo Juris Civilis Professore, Capite XXVII ejus Libri Scripti Anglica Sermone cui Titulum Fecit Compendium Legum Maritimarum.* It was discovered at the same time as the commentary *De Jure Praedae* and was published in 1872 in Muller's *Mare Clausum, Bijdrage tot de geschiedenis der rivaliteit van Engeland en Nederland in de zeventiende eeuw.*

> I have to observe, that two principles of public law are generally recognized as fundamental.
>
> One is the perfect equality and entire independence of all distinct states. Relative magnitude creates no distinction of right; relative imbecility, whether permanent or casual, gives no additional right to the more powerful neighbor; and any advantage seized upon that ground is mere usurpation. This is the great foundation of public law, which it mainly concerns the peace of mankind, both in their politic and private capacities, to preserve inviolate.
>
> The second is, that all nations being equal, all have an equal right to the uninterrupted use of the unappropriated parts of the ocean for their navigation. In places where no local authority exists, where the subjects of all states meet upon a footing of entire equality and independence, no one state, or any of its subjects, has a right to assume or exercise authority over the subjects of another.

In closing the preface to the *Mare Clausum,* Selden used language, which the undersigned quotes, albeit in an inverse sense, as a fit ending to this subject:

" Other passages there are everywhere of the same kind. But I enlarge myself too much in a thing so manifest. Therefore I forbear to light a candle to the sun. Farewell reader."

JAMES BROWN SCOTT,
Director of the Division of International Law.

WASHINGTON, D. C.,
February 28, 1916.

TRANSLATOR'S PREFACE

The Latin Text

The Latin Text is based upon the Elzevir edition of 1633, the modifications being only such as to bring the Latin into conformity with the present day Teubner and Oxford texts.

References in the notes to classic authors are given in unabbreviated form, following in other respects the Thesaurus Linguae Latinae Index. Citations to the Civil Law are given in the modern notation, which is followed, in parentheses, by the older method of reference. The text used is that of Mommsen, Krueger, Schoell et Kroll. The Canon Law is cited from the Friedberg edition of 1879-81. The abbreviations used are explained below.

The Translation

The translator wishes to make due acknowledgment for the passages from classic writers quoted from standard translations, to which references are also made in the notes. He has also consulted the French translation of Grotius by A. Guichon de Grandpont (1845). But his chief acknowledgment is to his colleague and friend, Professor Kirby Flower Smith of The Johns Hopkins University, to whom he read the translation, and who gave him the benefit of his knowledge of Latin and his taste in English, in a number of troublesome passages. Many niceties of the translation belong to Professor Smith, but mistakes in interpretation belong to the translator alone.

Acknowledgment and thanks are also due to Professor

Westel Woodbury Willoughby of Johns Hopkins, who has been so good as to read the translation through in galley proof and give the translator the benefit of his technical knowledge of law; to his Johns Hopkins colleague, Professor Wilfred P. Mustard, who has helped him out of a number of difficulties; to Bishop Shahan, Rector of the Catholic University of America, who has given of his time to help expand several of Grotius' abbreviated references to theological or canonical authors; to John Curlett Martin, Johns Hopkins Fellow in Greek, who has been of great assistance in the verification of references; and to the men of the Quinn and Boden Company for their courteous assistance while the book was going through the press.

List of Abbreviations

Auth., Authenticum.

Clem., Constitutiones Clementis Papae Quinti.

Dist., Distinctio Decreti Gratiani.

Extravag., Constitutiones XX D. Ioannis Papae XXII.

Lib. VI, Liber sextus Decretalium D. Bonifacii Papae VIII.

Other abbreviations should offer no difficulties.

Notes of Explanation

The words and phrases in the Latin text in capitals follow the type of the Elzevir text.

In order that both text and translation may be complete in themselves, the notes below the translation follow the notes of the text in shortened or expanded form, or in duplicate, as the occasion would seem to demand. The notes in Grotius' Latin text are in a most abbreviated form, and the references are seldom specific. They have been expanded without further explanation.

[ ] in the translation, text, or notes, inclose additions made by the translator.

CAPITA DISSERTATIONIS
HVGONIS GROTII DE MARE LIBERO

TABLE OF CONTENTS

AD

PRINCIPES

POPVLOSQVE LIBEROS

ORBIS CHRISTIANI

Error est non minus vetus quam pestilens, quo multi mortales, ii autem maxime qui plurimum vi atque opibus valent, persuadent sibi, aut, quod verius puto, persuadere conantur, iustum atque iniustum non suapte natura, sed hominum inani quadam opinione atque consuetudine distingui. Itaque illi et leges et aequitatis speciem in hoc inventa existimant, ut eorum qui in parendi condicione nati sunt dissensiones atque tumultus coerceantur; ipsis vero qui in summa fortuna sunt collocati, ius omne aiunt ex voluntate, voluntatem ex utilitate metiendam. Hanc autem sententiam absurdam plane atque naturae contrariam auctoritatis sibi nonnihil conciliasse haud adeo mirum est, cum ad morbum communem humani generis, quo sicut vitia ita vitiorum patrocinia sectamur, accesserint adulantium artes quibus omnis potestas obnoxia est.

Sed contra exstiterunt nullo non saeculo viri liberi, sapientes, religiosi, qui falsam hanc persuasionem animis simplicium evellerent ceteros autem eius defensores impudentiae convincerent. Deum quippe esse monstrabant conditorem rectoremque universi, imprimis autem humanae naturae parentem, quam ideo, non uti cetera animantia, in species diversas, variaque discrimina segregasset, sed unius esse generis, una etiam appellatione voluisset contineri,

TO THE RULERS AND TO THE FREE AND INDEPENDENT NATIONS OF CHRISTENDOM

The delusion is as old as it is detestable with which many men, especially those who by their wealth and power exercise the greatest influence, persuade themselves, or as I rather believe, try to persuade themselves, that justice and injustice are distinguished the one from the other not by their own nature, but in some fashion merely by the opinion and the custom of mankind. Those men therefore think that both the laws and the semblance of equity were devised for the sole purpose of repressing the dissensions and rebellions of those persons born in a subordinate position, affirming meanwhile that they themselves, being placed in a high position, ought to dispense all justice in accordance with their own good pleasure, and that their pleasure ought to be bounded only by their own view of what is expedient. This opinion, absurd and unnatural as it clearly is, has gained considerable currency; but this should by no means occasion surprise, inasmuch as there has to be taken into consideration not only the common frailty of the human race by which we pursue not only vices and their purveyors, but also the arts of flatterers, to whom power is always exposed.

But, on the other hand, there have stood forth in every age independent and wise and devout men able to root out this false doctrine from the minds of the simple, and to convict its advocates of shamelessness. For they showed that God was the founder and ruler of the universe, and especially that being the Father of all mankind, He had not separated human beings, as He had the rest of living things, into different species and various divisions, but had willed them to be of one race and to be known by one name; that

dedisset insuper originem eandem, similem membrorum compagem, vultus inter se obversos, sermonem quoque et alia communicandi instrumenta, ut intelligerent omnes naturalem inter se societatem esse atque cognationem. Huic autem a se fundatae aut domui aut civitati summum illum principem patremque familias suas quasdam scripsisse leges, non in aere aut tabulis, sed in sensibus animisque singulorum, ubi invitis etiam et aversantibus legendae occurrent his legibus summos pariter atque infimos teneri, in has non plus regibus licere, quam plebi adversus decreta decurionum, decurionibus contra praesidium edicta, praesidibus in regum ipsorum sanctiones. Quin illa ipsa populorum atque urbium singularum iura ex illo fonte dimanare, inde sanctimoniam suam atque maiestatem accipere.

Sicut autem in ipso homine alia sunt quae habet cum omnibus communia, alia quibus ab altero quisque distinguitur, ita earum rerum quas in usum hominis produxisset natura alias eam manere communes, alias cuiusque industria ac labore proprias fieri voluisse, de utrisque autem datas leges, ut communibus quidem sine detrimento omnium omnes uterentur, de ceteris autem quod cuique contigisset eo contentus abstineret alieno.

Haec si homo nullus nescire potest nisi homo esse desierit, haec si gentes viderunt quibus ad verum omne caecutientibus sola naturae fax illuxit, quid vos sentire ac facere aequum est, principes populique Christiani?

furthermore He had given them the same origin, the same structural organism, the ability to look each other in the face, language too, and other means of communication, in order that they all might recognize their natural social bond and kinship. They showed too that He is the supreme Lord and Father of this family; and that for the household or the state which He had thus founded, He had drawn up certain laws not graven on tablets of bronze or stone but written in the minds and on the hearts of every individual, where even the unwilling and the refractory must read them. That these laws were binding on great and small alike; that kings have no more power against them than have the common people against the decrees of the magistrates, than have the magistrates against the edicts of the governors, than have the governors against the ordinances of the kings themselves; nay more, that those very laws themselves of each and every nation and city flow from that Divine source, and from that source receive their sanctity and their majesty.

Now, as there are some things which every man enjoys in common with all other men, and as there are other things which are distinctly his and belong to no one else, just so has nature willed that some of the things which she has created for the use of mankind remain common to all, and that others through the industry and labor of each man become his own. Laws moreover were given to cover both cases so that all men might use common property without prejudice to any one else, and in respect to other things so that each man being content with what he himself owns might refrain from laying his hands on the property of others.

Now since no man can be ignorant of these facts unless he ceases to be a man, and since races blind to all truth except what they receive from the light of nature, have recognized their force, what, O Christian Kings and Nations, ought you to think, and what ought you to do?

Si quis durum putat ea a se exigi quae tam sancti nominis professio requirit, cuius minimum est ab iniuriis abstinere, certe quid sui sit offici scire quisque potest ex eo quod alteri praecipit. Nemo est vestrum qui non palam edicat rei quemque suae esse moderatorem et arbitrum: qui non fluminibus locisque publicis cives omnes uti ex aequo et promiscue iubeat, qui non commeandi commercandique libertatem omni ope defendat.

Sine his si parva illa societas, quam rempublicam vocamus, constare non posse iudicatur (et certe constare non potest) quamobrem non eadem illa ad sustinendam totius humani generis societatem atque concordiam erunt necessaria? Si quis adversus haec vim faciat, merito indignamini, exempla etiam pro flagiti magnitudine statuitis, non alia de causa nisi quia ubi ista passim licent status imperi tranquillus esse non potest. Quod si rex in regem, populus in populum inique et violente agat, id nonne ad perturbandam magnae illius civitatis quietem et ad summi custodis spectat iniuriam? Hoc interest, quod sicut magistratus minores de vulgo iudicant, vos de magistratibus, ita omnium aliorum delicta cognoscenda vobis et punienda mandavit rex universi, vestra excepit sibi. Is autem quamquam supremam animadversionem sibi reservat, tardam, occultam, inevitabilem, nihilominus duos a se iudices delegat qui rebus humanis intersint, quos nocentium felicissimus non effugit, conscientiam cuique suam, et famam sive existimationem

If any one thinks it hard that those things are demanded of him which the profession of a religion so sacred requires, the very least obligation of which is to refrain from injustice, certainly every one can know what his own duty is from the very demands he makes of others. There is not one of you who does not openly proclaim that every man is entitled to manage and dispose of his own property; there is not one of you who does not insist that all citizens have equal and indiscriminate right to use rivers and public places; not one of you who does not defend with all his might the freedom of travel and of trade.

If it be thought that the small society which we call a state cannot exist without the application of these principles (and certainly it cannot), why will not those same principles be necessary to uphold the social structure of the whole human race and to maintain the harmony thereof? If any one rebels against these principles of law and order you are justly indignant, and you even decree punishments in proportion to the magnitude of the offense, for no other reason than that a government cannot be tranquil where trespasses of that sort are allowed. If king act unjustly and violently against king, and nation against nation, such action involves a disturbance of the peace of that universal state, and constitutes a trespass against the supreme Ruler, does it not? There is however this difference: just as the lesser magistrates judge the common people, and as you judge the magistrates, so the King of the universe has laid upon you the command to take cognizance of the trespasses of all other men, and to punish them; but He has reserved for Himself the punishment of your own trespasses. But although He reserves to himself the final punishment, slow and unseen but none the less inevitable, yet He appoints to intervene in human affairs two judges whom the luckiest of sinners does not escape, namely, Conscience, or the innate estimation of oneself, and Public Opinion, or the estimation of others.

alienam. Haec tribunalia illis patent quibus alia praeclusa sunt; ad haec infirmi provocant; in his vincuntur qui vincunt viribus, qui licentiae modum non statuunt, qui vili putant constare quod emitur humano sanguine, qui iniurias iniuriis defendunt, quorum manifesta facinora necesse est et consentiente bonorum iudicio damnari, et sui ipsorum animi sententia non absolvi.

Ad utrumque hoc forum nos quoque novam causam afferimus; non hercule de stillicidiis aut tigno iniuncto, quales esse privatorum solent, ac ne ex eo quidem genere quod frequens est inter populos, de agri iure in confinio haerentis, de amnis aut insulae possessione; sed de omni prope oceano, de iure navigandi, de libertate commerciorum. Inter nos et Hispanos haec controversa sunt: Sitne immensum et vastum mare regni unius nec maximi accessio; populone cuiquam ius sit volentes populos prohibere ne vendant, ne permutent, ne denique commeent inter sese; potueritne quisquam quod suum numquam fuit elargiri, aut invenire quod iam erat alienum; an ius aliquod tribuat manifesta longi temporis iniuria.

In hac disceptatione ipsis qui inter Hispanos praecipui sunt divini atque humani iuris magistri calculum porrigimus, ipsius denique Hispaniae proprias leges imploramus. Id si nihil iuvat, et eos quos ratio certa convincit cupiditas vetat desistere, vestram principes maiestatem, vestram fidem quotquot estis ubique gentes appellamus.

Non perplexam, non intricatam movemus quaestionem. Non de ambiguis in religione capitibus, quae plurimum

These two tribunals are open to those who are debarred from all others; to these the powerless appeal; in them are defeated those who are wont to win by might, those who put no bounds to their presumption, those who consider cheap anything bought at the price of human blood, those who defend injustice by injustice, men whose wickedness is so manifest that they must needs be condemned by the unanimous judgment of the good, and cannot be cleared before the bar of their own souls.

To this double tribunal we bring a new case. It is in very truth no petty case such as private citizens are wont to bring against their neighbors about dripping eaves or party walls; nor is it a case such as nations frequently bring against one another about boundary lines or the possession of a river or an island. No! It is a case which concerns practically the entire expanse of the high seas, the right of navigation, the freedom of trade!! Between us and the Spaniards the following points are in dispute: Can the vast, the boundless sea be the appanage of one kingdom alone, and it not the greatest? Can any one nation have the right to prevent other nations which so desire, from selling to one another, from bartering with one another, actually from communicating with one another? Can any nation give away what it never owned, or discover what already belonged to some one else? Does a manifest injustice of long standing create a specific right?

In this controversy we appeal to those jurists among the Spanish themselves who are especially skilled both in divine and human law; we actually invoke the very laws of Spain itself. If that is of no avail, and those whom reason clearly convicts of wrong are induced by greed to maintain that stand, we invoke your majesty, ye Princes, your good faith, ye Peoples, whoever and wherever ye may be.

It is not an involved, it is not an intricate question that I am raising. It is not a question of ambiguous points of

habere videntur obscuritatis, quae tantis tam diu animis decertata, apud sapientes hoc fere certum reliquerunt, nusquam minus inveniri veritatem quam ubi cogitur assensus. Non de statu nostrae reipublicae, et libertate armis haud parta sed vindicata; de qua recte statuere ii demum possunt qui iura patria Belgarum, mores avitos, et institutum non in leges regnum, sed ex legibus principatum accurate cognoverint, in qua tamen quaestione aequis iudicibus extremae servitutis depulsa necessitas, subtilius inquirentibus decreti * tot nationum publica auctoritas, infensis etiam et malevolis adversariorum confessio nihil dubitandum reliquit.

Sed quod hic proponimus nihil cum istis commune habet, nullius indiget anxiae disquisitionis, non ex divini codicis pendet explicatione, cuius multa multi non capiunt, non ex unius populi scitis quae ceteri merito ignorant.

Lex illa e cuius praescripto iudicandum est, inventu est non difficilis, utpote eadem apud omnes; et facilis intellectu, utpote nata cum singulis, singulorum mentibus insita. Ius autem quod petimus tale est quod nec rex subditis negare debeat, neque Christianus non Christianis. A natura enim oritur, quae ex aequo omnium parens est, in omnes munifica, cuius imperium in eos extenditur qui gentibus imperant, et apud eos sanctissimum est qui in pietate plurimum profecerunt.

Cognoscite hanc causam principes! cognoscite populi! si quid iniquum postulamus, scitis quae vestra et e vobis eorum qui viciniores nobis estis apud nos semper fuerit auctoritas!

* [decreta (?); decreti is the reading of the 1633 and 1720 texts].

theology which seem to be wrapped in the deepest obscurity, which have been debated already so long and with such heat, that wise men are almost convinced that truth is never so rarely found as when assent thereto is forced. It is not a question of the status of our government and of independence not won by arms but restored. On this point those can reach a right decision who have an accurate knowledge of the ancestral laws and hereditary customs of the people of the Netherlands, and who have recognized that their state is not a kingdom illegally founded but is a government based upon law. In this matter, however, just judges no longer compelled to subordinate their convictions have been persuaded; the public authority of many nations has entirely satisfied those who were seeking a precedent; and the admissions of our adversaries have left even the foolish and malevolent no room for doubt.

But what I here submit has nothing in common with these matters. It calls for no troublesome investigation. It does not depend upon an interpretation of Holy Writ in which many people find many things they cannot understand, nor upon the decrees of any one nation of which the rest of the world very properly knows nothing.

The law by which our case must be decided is not difficult to find, seeing that it is the same among all nations; and it is easy to understand, seeing that it is innate in every individual and implanted in his mind. Moreover the law to which we appeal is one such as no king ought to deny to his subjects, and one no Christian ought to refuse to a non-Christian. For it is a law derived from nature, the common mother of us all, whose bounty falls on all, and whose sway extends over those who rule nations, and which is held most sacred by those who are most scrupulously just.

Take cognizance of this cause, ye Princes, take cognizance of it, ye Nations! If we are making an unjust demand, you know what your authority and the authority of

Monete, parebimus. Quin si quid a nobis hac in re peccatum est, iram vestram, odium denique humani generis non deprecamur. Sin contra se res habet, quid vobis censendum, quid agendum sit, vestrae religioni et aequitati relinquimus.

Olim inter populos humaniores summum nefas habebatur armis eos impetere qui res suas arbitris permitterent, contra qui tam aequam condicionem recusarent, ii non ut unius sed ut omnium hostes ope communi comprimebantur. Itaque eam in rem videmus icta foedera, iudices constitutos. Reges ipsi validaeque gentes nihil aeque gloriosum ac magnificum deputabant, quam aliorum coercere insolentiam, aliorum infirmitatem atque innocentiam sublevare. Qui si mos hodieque obtineret, ut humani nihil a se alienum * homines arbitrarentur, profecto orbe non paulo pacatiore uteremur; refrigesceret enim multorum audacia, et qui iustitiam utilitatis causa nunc negligunt, iniustitiam damno suo dediscerent.

Sed hoc ut in causa istac non frustra forte speramus, ita illud certo confidimus, bene rebus expensis existimaturos vos omnes imputari nobis non magis posse pacis moras, quam belli causas; ac proinde uti hactenus amici nobis faventes atque benevoli fuistis, ita vos aut etiam magis in posterum fore, quo nihil optatius iis potest contingere qui primam partem felicitatis putant bene facere, alteram bene audire.

* [Cf. Terence, Hautontimorumenos 77].

those of you who are our nearer neighbors has always been so far as we are concerned. Caution us, we will obey. Verily, if we have done any wrong in this our cause, we will not deprecate your wrath, nor even the hatred of the human race. But if we are right, we leave to your sense of righteousness and of fairness what you ought to think about this matter and what course of action you ought to pursue.

In ancient times among the more civilized peoples it was held to be the greatest of all crimes to make war upon those who were willing to submit to arbitration the settlement of their difficulties; but against those who declined so fair an offer all others turned, and with their combined resources overwhelmed them, not as enemies of any one nation, but as enemies of them all alike. So for this very object we see that treaties are made and arbiters appointed. Kings themselves and powerful nations used to think that nothing was so chivalrous or so noble as to coerce the insolent and to help the weak and innocent.

If today the custom held of considering that everything pertaining to mankind pertained also to one's self, we should surely live in a much more peaceable world. For the presumptuousness of many would abate, and those who now neglect justice on the pretext of expediency would unlearn the lesson of injustice at their own expense.

We have felt that perhaps we were not entertaining a foolish hope for our cause. At all events we are confident that you will all recognize after duly weighing the facts in the case that the delays to peace can no more be laid to our charge than can the causes of war; and as hitherto you have been indulgent, even favorably disposed to us, we feel sure that you will not only remain in this mind, but be even more friendly to us in the future. Nothing more to be desired than this can come to men who think that the first condition of happiness is good deeds; the second, good repute.

CAPVT I

Iure gentium quibusvis ad quosvis liberam esse navigationem

Propositum est nobis breviter ac dilucide demonstrare ius esse Batavis, hoc est, Ordinum Foederatorum Belgico-Germaniae subditis ad Indos, ita uti navigant navigare, cumque ipsis commercia colere. Fundamentum struemus hanc iuris gentium, quod primarium vocant regulam certissimam, cuius perspicua atque immutabilis est ratio; licere cuivis genti quamvis alteram adire, cumque ea negotiari.

Deus hoc ipse per naturam loquitur, cum ea cuncta quibus vita indiget, omnibus locis suppeditari a natura non vult: artibus etiam aliis alias gentes dat excellere. Quo ista, nisi quod voluit mutua egestate et copia humanas foveri amicitias, ne singuli se putantes sibi ipsis sufficere, hoc ipso redderentur insociabiles? Nunc factum est ut gens altera alterius suppleret inopiam, divinae iustitiae instituto, ut eo modo (sicut Plinius dicit[1]) quod genitum esset uspiam, apud omnes natum videretur. Poetas itaque canentes audimus:

Nec vero terrae ferre omnes omnia possunt.[2]

Item:

Excudent alii,

et quae sequuntur.[3]

[1] Panegyricus 29, 2: quod genitum esset usquam, id apud omnes natum esse videtur.

[2] Vergil, Georgica II, 109.

[3] Vergil, Aeneis VI, 847-853.

CHAPTER I

By the Law of Nations navigation is free to all persons whatsoever

My intention is to demonstrate briefly and clearly that the Dutch—that is to say, the subjects of the United Netherlands—have the right to sail to the East Indies, as they are now doing, and to engage in trade with the people there. I shall base my argument on the following most specific and unimpeachable axiom of the Law of Nations, called a primary rule or first principle, the spirit of which is self-evident and immutable, to wit: Every nation is free to travel to every other nation, and to trade with it.

God Himself says this speaking through the voice of nature; and inasmuch as it is not His will to have Nature supply every place with all the necessaries of life, He ordains that some nations excel in one art and others in another. Why is this His will, except it be that He wished human friendships to be engendered by mutual needs and resources, lest individuals deeming themselves entirely sufficient unto themselves should for that very reason be rendered unsociable? So by the decree of divine justice it was brought about that one people should supply the needs of another, in order, as Pliny the Roman writer says,[1] that in this way, whatever has been produced anywhere should seem to have been destined for all. Vergil also sings in this wise:

> "*Not every plant on every soil will grow,*"[2]

and in another place:

> "*Let others better mould the running mass*
> *Of metals,*" etc.[3]

[1] Panegyric 29, 2.

[2] Georgics II, 109 [Dryden's translation, II, 154].

[3] Aeneid VI, 847-853 [Dryden's translation, VI, 1168-1169].

Hoc igitur qui tollunt, illam laudatissimam tollunt humani generis societatem, tollunt mutuas benefaciendi occasiones, naturam denique ipsam violant. Nam et ille quem Deus terris circumfudit Oceanus, undique et undique versus navigabilis, et ventorum stati aut extraordinarii flatus, non ab eadem semper, et a nulla non aliquando regione spirantes, nonne significant satis concessum a natura cunctis gentibus ad cunctas aditum? Hoc Seneca [1] summum Naturae beneficium putat, quod et vento gentes locis dissipatas miscuit, et sua omnia in regiones ita descripsit, ut necessarium mortalibus esset inter ipsos commercium. Hoc igitur ius ad cunctas gentes aequaliter pertinet: quod clarissimi Iurisconsulti [2] eo usque producunt, ut negent ullam rempublicam aut Principem prohibere in universum posse, quo minus alii ad subditos suos accedant, et cum illis negotientur. Hinc ius descendit hospitale sanctissimum: hinc querelae:

Quod genus hoc hominum? quaeve hunc tam
barbara morem
Permittit patria? hospitio prohibemur harenae. [3]

Et alibi

. . . . . *litusque rogamus*
Innocuum et cunctis undamque auramque patentem. [4]

Et scimus bella quaedam ex hac causa coepisse, ut Me-

[1] Naturales Quaestiones III, IV.

[2] Institutes II, 1 (De rerum divisione, § 1); Digest 1, 8, 4 (eod. tit., L. Nemo igitur); cf. Gentilis, De jure belli I, 19; cf. Code IV, 63, 4 (De commerciis, L. Mercatores).

[3] Vergil, Aeneis I, 539-540.

[4] Vergil, Aeneis VII, 229-230.

Those therefore who deny this law, destroy this most praiseworthy bond of human fellowship, remove the opportunities for doing mutual service, in a word do violence to Nature herself. For do not the ocean, navigable in every direction with which God has encompassed all the earth, and the regular and the occasional winds which blow now from one quarter and now from another, offer sufficient proof that Nature has given to all peoples a right of access to all other peoples? Seneca [1] thinks this is Nature's greatest service, that by the wind she united the widely scattered peoples, and yet did so distribute all her products over the earth that commercial intercourse was a necessity to mankind. Therefore this right belongs equally to all nations. Indeed the most famous jurists [2] extend its application so far as to deny that any state or any ruler can debar foreigners from having access to their subjects and trading with them. Hence is derived that law of hospitality which is of the highest sanctity; hence the complaint of the poet Vergil:

> "*What men, what monsters, what inhuman race,*
> *What laws, what barbarous customs of the place,*
> *Shut up a desert shore to drowning men,*
> *And drive us to the cruel seas again.*" [3]

And:

> "*To beg what you without your want may spare—*
> *The common water, and the common air.*" [4]

We know that certain wars have arisen over this very matter; such for example as the war of the Megarians against the

[1] Natural Questions III, IV.

[2] Institutes II, 1; Digest I, 8, 4; cf. Gentilis, De jure belli I, 19; cf. Code IV, 63, 4 [Grotius refers particularly to his famous predecessor Albericus Gentilis (1552-1608), an Italian who came to England and was appointed to the chair of Regius Professor of Civil Law at Oxford. He published his De Jure Belli in 1588].

[3] Aeneid I, 539-540 [Dryden's translation, I, 760-763].

[4] Aeneid VII, 229-230 [Dryden's translation, VII, 313-314].

garensibus in Athenienses,[1] Bononiensibus in Venetos,[2] Castellanis etiam in Americanos has iustas potuisse belli causas esse, et ceteris probabiliores Victoria putat,[3] si peregrinari et degere apud illos prohiberentur, si arcerentur a participatione earum rerum quae iure gentium aut moribus communia sunt, si denique ad commercia non admitterentur.

Cui simile est quod in Mosis[4] historia et inde apud Augustinum legimus,[5] iusta bella Israelitas contra Amorrhaeos gessisse, quia innoxius transitus denegabatur; qui IVRE HVMANAE SOCIETATIS aequissimo patere debebat. Et hoc nomine Hercules Orchomeniorum, Graeci sub Agamemnone Mysorum Regi arma intulerunt,[6] quasi libera essent naturaliter itinera, ut Baldus dixit.[7] Accusan-

[1] Diodorus Siculus XI; Plutarch, Pericles XXIX, 4.

[2] Sigonius, De regno Italiae.

[3] Victoria, De Indis II, n. 1-7; Covarruvias, in c. Peccatum, § 9, n. 4, ibi Quinta.

[4] Numbers XXI, 21-26.

[5] Augustinus, Locutionum IV (de Numeris), 44; Et Estius, c. ult. 23, 4, 2.

[6] Sophocles, Trachiniae.

[7] Baldus de Ubaldis, Consilia III, 293.

Athenians,[1] and that of the Bolognese against the Venetians.[2] Again, Victoria [3] holds that the Spaniards could have shown just reasons for making war upon the Aztecs and the Indians in America, more plausible reasons certainly than were alleged, if they really were prevented from traveling or sojourning among those peoples, and were denied the right to share in those things which by the Law of Nations or by Custom are common to all, and finally if they were debarred from trade.

We read of a similar case in the history of Moses,[4] which we find mentioned also in the writings of Augustine,[5] where the Israelites justly smote with the edge of the sword the Amorites because they had denied the Israelites an innocent passage through their territory, a right which according to the Law of Human Society ought in all justice to have been allowed. In defense of this principle Hercules attacked the king of Orchomenus in Boeotia; and the Greeks under their leader Agamemnon waged war against the king of Mysia [6] on the ground that, as Baldus [7] has said, high roads were free

[1] Diodorus Siculus XI; Plutarch, Pericles XXIX, 4. [The Athenian decree prohibiting the Megarians from trading with Athens or any part of the Athenian Empire was one of the leading causes of the Peloponnesian War.]

[2] Carlo Sigonio [(1523-1584), an Italian humanist, in his work] On the Kingdom of Italy.

[3] Victoria, De Indis II, n. 1-7; Covarruvias, in c. Peccatum, § 9, n. 4, ibi Quinta [Franciscus de Victoria (1480-1546), the famous Spanish Scholastic, a Dominican, and Professor of Theology at Salamanca from 1521 until his death. His thirteen Relectiones (De Indis is no. V) were published ('vitiosa et corrupta') in 1557 after his death; the 1686 Cologne edition is held to be the best.

Diego Covarruvias (1512-1577), styled the Bartolo of Spain. He should probably be credited with formulating the reform decrees of the Council of Trent. The 5 vol. Antwerp 1762 edition of his works is the best.]

[4] Numbers XXI, 21-26.

[5] Locutionum IV (on Numbers), 44; Estius, c. ult. 23, 4, 2 [Estius (?-1613) was a Dutch commentator on the Epistles of St. Paul and on the works of St. Augustine].

[6] [Grotius refers to the Trachiniae of Sophocles, but probably from memory, for there is no such reference in that play.]

[7] Baldus de Ubaldis, Consilia III, 293 [Baldus (1327-1406) was a pupil of the great Bartolus].

turque a Germanis apud Tacitum[1] Romani, quod colloquia congressusque gentium arcerent, fluminaque et terras et coelum quodam modo ipsum clauderent. Nec ullus titulus Christianis quondam in Saracenos magis placuit, quam quod per illos terrae Iudaeae aditu arcerentur.[2]

Sequitur ex sententia Lusitanos etiamsi domini essent earum regionum ad quas Batavi proficiscuntur, iniuriam tamen facturos si aditum Batavis et mercatum praecluderent.

Quanto igitur iniquius est volentes aliquos a volentium populorum commercio secludi, illorum opera quorum in potestate nec populi isti sunt, nec illud ipsum, qua iter est, quando latrones etiam et piratas non alio magis nomine detestamur, quam quod illi hominum inter se commeatus obsident atque infestant?

[1] Tacitus, Historiae IV, 64.

[2] Andreas Alciatus, Commentaria VII, 130; Covarruvias in c. Peccatum, p. 2 § 9; Bartolus on Code I, 11 (De paganis, L. 1).

by nature. Again, as we read in Tacitus,[1] the Germans accused the Romans of 'preventing all intercourse between them and of closing up to them the rivers and roads, and almost the very air of heaven'. When in days gone by the Christians made crusades against the Saracens, no other pretext was so welcome or so plausible as that they were denied by the infidels free access to the Holy Land.[2]

It follows therefore that the Portuguese, even if they had been sovereigns in those parts to which the Dutch make voyages, would nevertheless be doing them an injury if they should forbid them access to those places and from trading there.

Is it not then an incalculably greater injury for nations which desire reciprocal commercial relations to be debarred therefrom by the acts of those who are sovereigns neither of the nations interested, nor of the element over which their connecting high road runs? Is not that the very cause which for the most part prompts us to execrate robbers and pirates, namely, that they beset and infest our trade routes?

[1] Histories IV, 64 [In connection with the revolt of Civilis].

[2] Andrea Alciati, Commentaria VII, 130; Covarruvias in c. Peccatum, p. 2 § 9; Bartolus on Code I, 11 [Alciati (1492-1550) was made Comes Palatinus by the Emperor Charles V, and offered a Cardinal's hat by Pope Paul III, which he refused, but he did become a Protonotarius Apostolicus].

CAPVT II

Lusitanos nullum habere ius dominii in eos Indos ad quos Batavi navigant titulo inventionis

Non esse autem Lusitanos earum partium dominos ad quas Batavi accedunt, puta Iavae, Taprobanae, partis maximae Moluccarum, certissimo argumento colligimus, quia dominus nemo est eius rei quam nec ipse umquam nec alter ipsius nomine possedit. Habent insulae istae quas dicimus et semper habuerunt suos reges, suam rempublican, suas leges, sua iura; Lusitanis mercatus, ut aliis gentibus conceditur; itaque et tributa cum pendunt, et ius mercandi a principibus exorant, dominos se non esse, sed ut externos advenire satis testantur; ne habitant quidem nisi precario. Et quamquam ad dominium titulus non sufficiat, quia et possessio requiritur, cum aliud sit rem habere, aliud ius ad rem consequendam, tamen ne titulum quidem dominii in eas partes Lusitanis ullum esse affirmo, quem non ipsis eripuerit Doctorum, et quidem Hispanorum sententia.

Primum si dicent inventionis praemio eas terras sibi cessisse, nec ius, nec verum dicent. Invenire enim non illud est oculis usurpare, sed apprehendere, ut Gordiani epistola

CHAPTER II

The Portuguese have no right by title of discovery to sovereignty over the East Indies to which the Dutch make voyages

The Portuguese are not sovereigns of those parts of the East Indies to which the Dutch sail, that is to say, Java, Ceylon,* and many of the Moluccas. This I prove by the incontrovertible argument that no one is sovereign of a thing which he himself has never possessed, and which no one else has ever held in his name. These islands of which we speak, now have and always have had their own kings, their own government, their own laws, and their own legal systems. The inhabitants allow the Portuguese to trade with them, just as they allow other nations the same privilege. Therefore, inasmuch as the Portuguese pay tolls, and obtain leave to trade from the rulers there, they thereby give sufficient proof that they do not go there as sovereigns but as foreigners. Indeed they only reside there on sufferance. And although the title to sovereignty is not sufficient, inasmuch as possession is a prerequisite—for having a thing is quite different from having the right to acquire it—nevertheless I affirm that in those places the Portuguese have no title at all to sovereignty which is not denied them by the opinion of learned men, even of the Spaniards.

First of all, if they say that those lands have come under their jurisdiction as the reward of discovery, they lie, both in law and in fact. For to discover a thing is not only to seize it with the eyes but to take real possession thereof,

* [Taprobane was the ancient name of Ceylon. Milton speaks of it in Paradise Regained IV, 75:

"And utmost Indian Isle Taprobane."]

ostenditur;[1] unde Grammatici[2] invenire et occupare pro verbis ponunt idem significantibus; et tota Latinitas quod adepti sumus, id demum invenisse nos dicit, cui oppositum est perdere. Quin et ipsa naturalis ratio, et legum diserta verba, et eruditiorum interpretatio[3] manifeste ostendit, ad titulum dominii parandum eam demum sufficere inventionem quae cum possessione coniuncta est, ubi scilicet res mobiles apprehenduntur, aut immobiles terminis atque custodia sepiuntur;[4] quod in hac specie dici nullo modo potest. Nam praesidia illic Lusitani nulla habent. Quid quod ne reperisse quidem Indiam ullo modo dici possunt Lusitani, quae tot a saeculis fuerat celeberrima. Iam ab Horati tempore:[5]

Impiger extremos currit mercator ad Indos
Per mare pauperiem fugiens.

Taprobanes pleraque quam exacte nobis Romani descripsere?[6] Iam vero et ceteras insulas ante Lusitanos non

[1] Code VIII, 40, 13 (De fideiussoribus, L. Si Barsagoram).

[2] Nonius Marcellus, De varia significatione sermonum, in verbo 'occupare' (p. 562, Lindsay); cf. Connanus, Commentarii juris civilis III, 3; cf. Donellus Commentarii de jure civili IV, 10.

[3] Institutes II, 1, 13 (De rerum divisione, § Illud quaesitum est).

[4] Digest XLI, 2, 3 (De adquirenda possessione, § Neratius).

[5] Epistulae I, 1, 44-45.

[6] Pliny, Naturalis historia VI, 22.

as Gordian [1] points out in one of his letters. For that reason the Grammarians [2] give the same signification to the expressions 'to find' and 'to occupy'; and all Latinity applies the phrase 'we have found' only to the thing which 'we have seized'; and the opposite of this is 'to lose'. However, natural reason itself, the precise words of the law, and the interpretation of the more learned men [3] all show clearly that the act of discovery is sufficient to give a clear title of sovereignty only when it is accompanied by actual possession. And this only applies of course to movables or to such immovables as are actually inclosed within fixed bounds and guarded.[4] No such claim can be established in the present case, because the Portuguese maintain no garrisons in those regions. Neither can the Portuguese by any possible means claim to have discovered India, a country which was famous centuries and centuries ago! It was already known as early as the time of the emperor Augustus as the following quotation from Horace shows:

> "*That worst of evils, poverty, to shun*
> *Dauntless through seas, and rocks, and fires you run*
> *To furthest Ind,*" [5]

And have not the Romans described for us in the most exact way the greater part of Ceylon? [6] And as far as the other islands are concerned, not only the neighboring

[1] Code VIII, 40, 13 [Probably Fabius Claudius Gordianus Fulgentius (468-533), a Benedictine monk, one of the Latin Fathers].

[2] Nonius Marcellus, On the various significations of speech, under the word 'occupare'; cf. Connan, Commentaries on the civil law III, 3; Donellus [Doneau], Commentaries on the civil law IV, 10. [François de Connan (1508-1551), a French jurisconsult, a pupil of Alciati; Hugues Doneau (1527-1591) a famous jurisconsult, who wrote many volumes of commentaries on the Digest and the Code.]

[3] Institutes II, 1, 13.

[4] Digest XLI, 2, 3.

[5] Letters I, 1, 44-45 [Francis's translation, English Poets XIX, 726].

[6] Pliny, Natural History, VI, 22.

finitimi tantum Persae et Arabes, sed Europaei etiam, praecipue Veneti noverant.

Praeterea inventio nihil iuris tribuit, nisi in ea quae ante inventionem nullius fuerant.[1] Atqui Indi cum ad eos Lusitani venerunt, etsi partim idololatrae, partim Mahumetani erant, gravibusque peccatis involuti, nihilominus publice atque privatim rerum possessionumque suarum dominium habuerunt, quod illis sine iusta causa eripi non potuit.[2] Ita certissimis rationibus post alios auctores maximi nominis concludit Hispanus Victoria:[3] 'Non possunt', inquit, 'Christiani saeculares aut Ecclesiastici potestate civili et principatu privare infideles, eo dumtaxat titulo, quia infideles sunt, nisi ab eis alia iniuria profecta sit'.

Fides enim, ut recte inquit Thomas[4] non tollit ius naturale aut humanum ex quo dominia profecta sunt. Immo credere infideles non esse rerum suarum dominos, haereticum est; et res ab illis possessas illis ob hoc ipsum eripere furtum est et rapina, non minus quam si idem fiat Christianis.

Recte igitur dicit Victoria[5] non magis ista ex causa Hispanis ius in Indos quaesitum, quam Indis fuisset in Hispanos, si qui illorum priores in Hispaniam venissent. Neque vero sunt Indi Orientis amentes et insensati, sed

[1] Digest XLI, 1, 3 (De adquirendo rerum dominio).
[2] Covarruvias in c. Peccatum § 10, n. 2, 4, 5.
[3] De potestate civili I, 9.
[4] Thomas Aquinas, Summa II. II, q. 10, a. 12.
[5] De Indis I, n. 4-7, 19.

Persians and Arabs, but even Europeans, particularly the Venetians, knew them long before the Portuguese did.

But in addition to all this, discovery *per se* gives no legal rights over things unless before the alleged discovery they were *res nullius*.[1] Now these Indians of the East, on the arrival of the Portuguese, although some of them were idolators, and some Mohammedans, and therefore sunk in grievous sin, had none the less perfect public and private ownership of their goods and possessions, from which they could not be dispossessed without just cause.[2] The Spanish writer Victoria,[3] following other writers of the highest authority, has the most certain warrant for his conclusion that Christians, whether of the laity or of the clergy, cannot deprive infidels of their civil power and sovereignty merely on the ground that they are infidels, unless some other wrong has been done by them.

For religious belief, as Thomas Aquinas[4] rightly observes, does not do away with either natural or human law from which sovereignty is derived. Surely it is a heresy to believe that infidels are not masters of their own property; consequently, to take from them their possessions on account of their religious belief is no less theft and robbery than it would be in the case of Christians.

Victoria then is right in saying[5] that the Spaniards have no more legal right over the East Indians because of their religion, than the East Indians would have had over the Spaniards if they had happened to be the first foreigners to come to Spain. Nor are the East Indians stupid and unthinking; on the contrary they are intelligent and shrewd,

[1] Digest XLI, 1, 3.

[2] Covarruvias in c. Peccatum § 10, n. 2, 4, 5.

[3] De potestate civili I, 9.

[4] Summa II. II, q. 10, a. 12 [Thomas Aquinas (1227-1274), one of the most famous of the Schoolmen and Theologians, spoken of often as Aquila Theologorum, and Doctor Angelicus].

[5] De Indis I, n. 4-7, 19.

ingeniosi et solertes, ita ut ne hinc quidem praetextus subiciendi possit desumi, qui tamen per se satis est manifestae iniquitatis. Iam olim Plutarchus πρόφασιν πλεονεξίας fuisse dicit ἡμερῶσαι τὰ βαρβαρικά,* improbam scilicet alieni cupiditatem hoc sibi velum obtendere, quod barbariem mansuefacit. Et nunc etiam color ille redigendi invitas gentes ad mores humaniores, qui Graecis olim et Alexandro usurpatus est, a Theologis omnibus, praesertim Hispanis,[1] improbus atque impius censetur.

[1] Vasquius, Preface (n. 5) to Controversiae illustres.

* [Plutarch, Pompeius LXX].

so that a pretext for subduing them on the ground of their character could not be sustained. Such a pretext on its very face is an injustice. Plutarch said long ago that the civilizing of barbarians had been made the pretext for aggression, which is to say that a greedy longing for the property of another often hides itself behind such a pretext. And now that well-known pretext of forcing nations into a higher state of civilization against their will, the pretext once seized by the Greeks and by Alexander the Great,* is considered by all theologians, especially those of Spain,[1] to be unjust and unholy.

[1] Vasquius, Preface (n. 5) to Controversiae illustres.

* [Cf. Plutarch, Of the Fortune or Virtue of Alexander the Great I, 5].

CAPVT III

Lusitanos in Indos non habere ius dominii titulo donationis Pontificiae

Secundo si Pontificis Alexandri Sexti divisione utentur, ante omnia illud attendendum est, volueritne Pontifex contentiones tantum Lusitanorum et Castellanorum dirimere, quod potuit sane, ut lectus inter illos arbiter, sicut et ipsi Reges iam ante inter se ea de re foedera quaedam pepigerant;[1] et hoc si ita est, cum res inter alios acta sit, ad ceteras gentes non pertinebit; an vero prope singulos mundi trientes duobus populis donare. Quod etsi voluisset, et potuisset Pontifex, non tamen continuo sequeretur dominos eorum locorum esse Lusitanos, cum donatio dominum non faciat, sed secuta traditio;[2] quare et huic causae possessio deberet accedere.

Tum vero si quis ius ipsum sive divinum sive humanum scrutari volet, non autem ex commodo suo metiri, facile

[1] Cf. Osorium.
[2] Institutes II, 1, 40 (De rerum divisione, § Per traditionem).

CHAPTER III

The Portuguese have no right of sovereignty over the East Indies by virtue of title based on the Papal Donation

Next, if the partition made by the Pope Alexander VI * is to be used by the Portuguese as authority for jurisdiction in the East Indies, then before all things else two points must be taken into consideration.

First, did the Pope merely desire to settle the disputes between the Portuguese and the Spaniards?

This was clearly within his power, inasmuch as he had been chosen to arbitrate between them, and in fact the kings of both countries had previously concluded certain treaties with each other on this very matter.[1] Now if this be the case, seeing that the question concerns only the Portuguese and Spaniards, the decision of the Pope will of course not affect the other peoples of the world.

Second, did the Pope intend to give to two nations, each one third of the whole world?

But even if the Pope had intended and had had the power to make such a gift, still it would not have made the Portuguese sovereigns of those places. For it is not a donation that makes a sovereign, it is the consequent delivery of a thing [2] and the subsequent possession thereof.

Now, if any one will scrutinize either divine or human law, not merely with a view to his own interests, he will

[1] [Grotius cites Osorius, but gives no reference.]

[2] Institutes II, 1, 40.

* [The Cambridge Modern History, I, 23-24, has a good paragraph upon this famous Papal Bull of May 14, 1493 (modified June 7, 1494, by treaty of Tordesillas).]

deprehendet donationem eiusmodi ut rei alienae nullius esse momenti. Disputationem de potestate Pontificis, hoc est Episcopi Romanae Ecclesiae, hic non aggrediar, nec quicquam ponam nisi ex hypothesi, hoc est, quod confitentur homines inter eos eruditissimi, qui plurimum Pontificiae tribuunt auctoritati, maxime Hispani, qui cum pro sua perspicacia facile vident Dominum Christum omne a se terrenum imperium abdicasse,[1] mundi certe totius dominium, qua homo fuit, non habuisse, et si habuisset, nullis tamen argumentis astrui posse ius illud in Petrum, aut Romanam Ecclesiam Vicarii iure translatum; cum alias etiam certum sit, multa Christum habuisse in quae Pontifex non successerit,[2] intrepide affirmarunt (utar ipsorum verbis) Pontificem non esse dominum civilem aut temporalem totius orbis.[3] Immo etiam si quam talem potestatem in mundo haberet, eam tamen non recte exerciturum, cum spirituali sua iurisdictione contentus esse debeat, saecularibus autem Principibus eam concedere nullo modo posse. Tum vero si quam habeat potestatem, eam habere, ut loquuntur in ordine ad spiritualia.[4] Quocirca nullam illi esse potestatem in populos infideles, ut qui ad Ecclesiam non pertineant.[5]

Vnde sequitur ex sententia Caietani et Victoriae et

[1] Luke XII, 14; John XVIII, 36; Victoria, De Indis I, n. 25.

[2] Victoria XVI, n. 27.

[3] Vasquius, Controversiae illustres, c. 21; Turre Cremata II, c. 113; Hugo on Dist. XCVI, C. VI (Cum ad verum); Bernhardus, De consolatione ad Eugenium II; Victoria, De Indis I, n. 27; Covarruvias in c. Peccatum § 9, n. 7.

[4] Matthew XVII, 27; XX, 26; John VI, 15.

[5] Victoria, De Indis I, n. 28, 30; Covarruvias on I Corinthians V in fine; Thomas Aquinas, Summa II. II, q. 12, a. 2; Ayala, De Jure I, 2, 29.

easily apprehend that a donation of this kind, dealing with the property of others, is of no effect. I shall not enter here upon any discussion as to the power of the Pope, that is the Bishop of the Roman Church, nor shall I advance anything but a hypothesis which is accepted by men of the greatest erudition, who lay the greatest stress on the power of the Pope, especially the Spaniards, who with their perspicacity easily see that our Lord Jesus Christ when he said "My kingdom is not of this world" thereby renounced all earthly power,[1] and that while He was on earth as a man, He certainly did not have dominion over the whole world, and if He had had such dominion, still by no arguments could such a right be transferred to Peter, or be transmitted to the Roman Church by authority of the 'Vicar of Christ'; indeed, inasmuch as Christ had many things to which the Pope did not succeed,[2] it has been boldly affirmed—and I shall use the very words of the writers—that the Pope is neither civil nor temporal Lord of the whole world.[3] On the contrary, even if the Pope did have any such power on earth, still he would not be right in using it, because he ought to be satisfied with his own spiritual jurisdiction, and be utterly unable to grant that power to temporal princes. So then, if the Pope has any power at all, he has it, as they say, in the spiritual realm only.[4] Therefore he has no authority over infidel nations, for they do not belong to the Church.[5]

It follows therefore according to the opinions of

[1] Luke XII, 14; John XVIII, 36; Victoria, De Indis I, n. 25.

[2] Victoria XVI, n. 27.

[3] Vasquius, Controversiae illustres, c. 21; Torquemada II, c. 113; Hugo on Dist. XCVI, C. VI; St. Bernard, Admonitory epistle to Pope Eugene III, book 2; Victoria, De Indis I, n. 27; Covarruvias in c. Peccatum § 9, n. 7.

[4] Matthew XVII, 27; XX, 26; John VI, 15.

[5] Victoria, De Indis I, n. 28, 30; Covarruvias on I Corinthinas V, at the end; Thomas Aquinas, Summa II. II, q. 12, a. 2; Ayala, De Jure I, 2, 29 [Best edition of Ayala is in The Classics of International Law, Carnegie Institution of Washington, 2 vol., 1912].

potioris partis tam Theologorum quam Canonistarum,[1] non esse idoneum titulum adversus Indos, vel quia Papa dederit provincias illas tamquam dominus absolute, vel quia non recognoscunt dominium Papae; atque adeo ne Saracenos quidem isto titulo umquam spoliatos.

[1] Thomas Aquinas, Summa II. II, q. 66, a. 8; Silvius, De infidelibus § 7; Innocentius on Decretales Gregorii Papae IX, III, 34, 8 (De voto, c. Quod super his); Victoria, De Indis I, n. 31.

Cajetan and Victoria and the more authoritative of the Theologians and writers on Canon Law,[1] that there is no clear title against the East Indians, based either on the ground that the Pope made an absolute grant of those provinces as if he were their sovereign, or on the pretext that the East Indians do not recognize his sovereignty. Indeed, and in truth, it may be affirmed that no such pretext as that was ever invoked to despoil even the Saracens.

[1] Thomas Aquinas, Summa II. II, q. 66, a. 8; Silvius, De infidelibus § 7; Innocent on the Decretals of Pope Gregory IX, III, 34, 8; Victoria, De Indis I, n. 31. [Franciscus Silvius, or Sylvius, or du Bois (1581-1649), was a Belgian theologian.]

CAPVT IV

Lusitanos in Indos non habere ius dominii titulo belli

His igitur sublatis cum manifestum sit, quod et Victoria scribit,[1] Hispanos ad terras remotiores illas navigantes nullum ius secum attulisse occupandi eas provincias, unus dumtaxat titulus belli restat, qui et ipse si iustus esset, tamen ad dominium proficere non posset, nisi iure praedae, hoc est post occupationem. Atqui tantum abest ut Lusitani eas res occupaverint, ut cum plerisque gentibus quas Batavi accesserunt, bellum eo tempore nullum haberent. Et sic igitur nullum ius illis quaeri potuit, cum etiam si quas ab Indis pertulissent iniurias, eas longa pace et amicis commerciis remisisse merito censeantur.

Quamquam ne fuit quidem quod bello obtenderent. Nam qui Barbaros bello persequuntur ut Americanos Hispani, duo solent praetexere, quod ab illis commercio arceantur, aut quod doctrinam verae religionis illi nolent agnoscere. Et commercia quidem Lusitani ab Indis impetrarunt,[2] ut hac in parte nihil habeant quod querantur.

[1] De Indis I, n. 31.
[2] Vasquius, Controversiae illustres, c. 24; Victoria, De Indis II, n. 10.

CHAPTER IV

The Portuguese have no right of sovereignty over the East Indies by title of war

Since it is clear, (as Victoria also says),[1] from the refutation of any claim to title from the Pope's Donation, that the Spaniards when they sailed to those distant lands did not carry with them any right to occupy them as provinces, only one kind of title remains to be considered, namely, that based upon war. But even if this title could be justified, it would not serve to establish sovereignty, except by right of conquest, that is to say, occupation would be a prerequisite. But the Portuguese were as far as possible from occupation of those lands. They were not even at war with most of the peoples whom the Dutch visited. So therefore no legal claim could be established there by the Portuguese, because even if they had suffered wrongs from the East Indians, it might reasonably be considered by the long peace and friendly commercial relations that those injuries had been forgiven.

Indeed there was no pretext at all for going to war. For those who force war upon barbarous peoples, as the Spaniards did upon the aborigines of America, commonly allege one of two pretexts: either that they have been refused the right to trade, or that the barbarians are unwilling to acknowledge the doctrines of the True Faith. But as the Portuguese actually obtained from the East Indians the right to trade,[2] they have, on that score at least, no

[1] De Indis I, n. 31.

[2] Vasquius, Controversiae illustres, c. 24; Victoria, De Indis II, n. 10.

Alter vero obtentus nihilo est iustior, quam ille Graecorum in Barbaros, quo Boëthius respexit: [1]

An distant quia dissidentque mores,
Iniustas acies, et fera bella movent,
Alternisque volunt perire telis?
Non est iusta satis saevitiae ratio.

Ista autem et Thomae et Concili Toletani et Gregori et Theologorum, Canonistarum, Iurisprudentiumque fere omnium conclusio est: [2] Quantumcumque fides annuntiata sit Barbaris (nam de his qui subditi ante fuerunt Christianis Principibus item de Apostatis alia est quaestio) probabiliter et sufficienter, et si noluerint eam respicere, non tamen licere hac ratione eos bello persequi, et spoliare bonis suis.[3]

Operae pretium est in hanc rem ipsa Caietani verba describere: [4] 'Quidam', ait, 'infideles nec de iure nec de facto subsunt secundum temporalem iurisdictionem Principibus Christianis, ut inveniuntur pagani, qui numquam imperio Romano subditi fuerunt, terras habitantes, in quibus Christianum numquam fuit nomen. Horum namque domini, quamvis infideles, legitimi domini sunt, sive regali sive politico regimine gubernantur; nec sunt propter infidelitatem a dominio suorum privati, cum dominium sit

[1] De consolatione philosophiae IV, carmen 4, 7-10.
[2] Thomas Aquinas, Summa II. II, q. 10, a. 8; Dist. XLV, C. V (De Iudeis), C. III (Qui sincera); Innocentius, cf. note 1, page 17; Bartolus on Code I, 11, 1 (De paganis); Covarruvias in c. Peccatum, § 9, 10; Ayala, De Jure I, 2, 28.
[3] Matthew X, 23.
[4] On Thomas Aquinas, Summa II. II, q. 4, 66, a. 8.

grounds of complaint. Nor is there any better justification for the other pretext than the one alleged by the Greeks against the barbarians, to which Boëthius makes the following allusion:

"*Unjust and cruel wars they wage,*
And haste with flying darts the death to meet or deal.
No right nor reason can they show;
'Tis but because their lands and laws are not the same."[1]

Moreover the verdict of Thomas Aquinas, of the Council of Toledo, of Gregory, and of nearly all theologians, canonists, and jurists, is as follows:[2] However persuasively and sufficiently the True Faith has been preached to the heathen —former subjects of Christian princes or apostates are quite another question—if they are unwilling to heed it, that is not sufficient cause to justify war upon them, or to despoil them of their goods.[3]

It is worth while on this point to quote the actual words of Cajetan:[4] 'There are some infidels who are neither in law nor in fact under the temporal jurisdiction of Christian princes; just as there were pagans who were never subjects of the Roman Empire, and yet who inhabit lands where the name of Christ was never heard. Now their rulers, though heathen, are legitimate rulers, whether the people live under a monarchical or a democratic régime. They are not to be deprived of sovereignty over their pos-

[1] On the Consolation of Philosophy IV, 4, 7-10 [H. R. James' translation, page 194].

[2] Thomas Aquinas, Summa II. II, q. 10, a. 8; Dist. XLV, C. V, C. III; Innocent, see note 1, page 17; Bartolus on Code I, 11, 1; Covarruvias in c. Peccatum, § 9, 10; Ayala, De Jure I, 2, 28.

[3] Matthew X, 23.

[4] On Thomas Aquinas, Summa II. II, q. 4, 66, a. 8 [Thomas de Cajetan (1469-1534), an Italian cardinal, wrote voluminous commentaries on Thomas Aquinas, Aristotle, and the Bible].

ex iure positivo, et infidelitas ex divino iure, quod non tollit ius positivum, ut superius in quaestione habitum est. Et de his nullam scio legem quoad temporalia. Contra hos nullus Rex, nullus Imperator, nec Ecclesia Romana potest movere bellum ad occupandas terras eorum, aut subiciendos illos temporaliter; quia nulla subest causa iusta belli, cum Iesus Christus Rex Regum, cui data est potestas in caelo et in terra, miserit ad capiendam possessionem mundi, non milites armatae militiae, sed sanctos praedicatores, sicut oves inter lupos. Vnde nec in testamento veteri, ubi armata manu possessio erat capienda, terrae infidelium inductum lego bellum alicui propter hoc quod non erant fideles, sed quia nolebant dare transitum, vel quia eos offenderant, ut Madianitae, vel ut recuperarent sua, divina largitate sibi concessa. Vnde GRAVISSIME PECCAREMVS, si fidem Christi Iesu per hanc viam ampliare contenderemus; nec essemus LEGITIMI DOMINI illorum, sed MAGNA LATROCINIA committeremus, et teneremur ad restitutionem, utpote INIVSTI DEBELLATORES AVT OCCVPATORES. Mittendi essent ad hos praedicatores boni viri, qui verbo et exemplo converterent eos ad Deum; et non qui eos opprimant, spolient, scandalizent, subiciant, et duplo gehennae filios faciant, more Pharisaeorum '.

Et in hanc formam audimus saepe a Senatu in Hispania, et Theologis praecipue Dominicanis decretum fuisse, sola verbi praedicatione non bello Americanos ad fidem traducendos; libertatem etiam quae illis eo nomine erepta esset,

sessions because of their unbelief, since sovereignty is a matter of positive law, and unbelief is a matter of divine law, which cannot annul positive law, as has been argued above. In fact I know of no law against such unbelievers as regards their temporal possessions. Against them no King, no Emperor, not even the Roman Church, can declare war for the purpose of occupying their lands, or of subjecting them to temporal sway. For there is no just cause for war, since Jesus Christ the King of Kings, to whom all power was given in heaven and on earth, sent out for the conquest of the world not armed soldiers, but holy disciples, "as sheep in the midst of wolves." Nor do I read in the Old Testament, when possession had to be obtained by force of arms, that the Israelites waged war on any heathen land because of the unbelief of its inhabitants; but it was because the heathen refused them the right of innocent passage, or attacked them, as the Midianites did; or it was to recover the possessions which had been bestowed upon them by divine bounty. Wherefore we should be most miserable sinners if we should attempt to extend the religion of Jesus Christ by such means. Nor should we be their lawful rulers, but, on the contrary, we should be committing great robberies, and be compelled to make restitution as unjust conquerors and invaders. There must be sent to them as preachers, good men to convert them to God by their teaching and example; not men who will oppress them, despoil them, subdue and proselytize them, and "make them twofold more the children of hell than themselves," * after the manner of the Pharisees'.

Indeed I have often heard that it has been decreed by the Council of Spain, and by the Churchmen, especially the Dominicans, that the Americans (Aztecs and Indians) should be converted to the Faith by the preaching of the Word alone, and not by war, and even that their liberty of

* Matthew XXIII, 15.

restitui debere, quod a Paulo tertio Pontifice, et Carolo V Imperatore Hispaniarum Rege comprobatum dicitur.

Omittimus iam Lusitanos in plerisque partibus religionem nihil promovere, ne operam quidem dare, cum soli lucro invigilent. Immo et illud ibi verum esse, quod de Hispanis in America Hispanus scripsit, non miracula, non signa audiri, non exempla vitae religiosae, quae ad eandem fidem alios possent impellere, sed multa scandala, multa facinora, multas impietates.

Quare cum et possessio et titulus deficiat possessionis, neque res dicionesque Indorum pro talibus haberi debeant quasi nullius ante fuissent, neque cum illorum essent, ab aliis recte acquiri potuerint, sequitur Indorum populos, de quibus nos loquimur, Lusitanorum proprios non esse, sed liberos, et sui iuris; de quo ipsi doctores Hispani non dubitant.[1]

[1] Victoria, De Indis II, 1.

which they had been robbed in the name of religion should be restored. This policy is said to have received the approval of Pope Paul III, and of Emperor Charles V, King of the Spains.

I pass over the fact that the Portuguese in most places do not further the extension of the faith, or indeed, pay any attention to it at all, since they are alive only to the acquisition of wealth. Nay, the very thing that is true of them, is the very thing which has been written of the Spaniards in America by a Spaniard, namely, that nothing is heard of miracles or wonders or examples of devout and religious life such as might convert others to the same faith, but on the other hand no end of scandals, of crimes, of impious deeds.

Wherefore, since both possession and a title of possession are lacking, and since the property and the sovereignty of the East Indies ought not to be considered as if they had previously been *res nullius,* and since, as they belong to the East Indians, they could not have been acquired legally by other persons, it follows that the East Indian nations in question are not the chattels of the Portuguese, but are free men and *sui juris.* This is not denied even by the Spanish jurists themselves.[1]

[1] Victoria, De Indis II, 1.

CAPVT V

Mare ad Indos aut ius eo navigandi non esse proprium Lusitanorum titulo occupationis

Si ergo in populos terrasque et diciones Lusitani ius nullum quaesiverunt, videamus an mare et navigationem, aut mercaturam sui iuris facere potuerint. De mari autem prima sit consideratio, quod cum passim in iure aut nullius, aut commune, aut publicum iuris gentium dicatur, hae voces quid significent ita commodissime explicabitur, si Poetas ab Hesiodo omnes, et Philosophos; et Iurisconsultos veteres imitati in tempora distinguamus, ea, quae tempore forte haud longo, certa tamen ratione, et sui natura discreta sunt. Neque nobis vitio verti debet si in iuris a natura procedentis explicatione auctoritate et verbis eorum utimur quos constat naturali iudicio plurimum valuisse.

Sciendum est igitur in primordiis vitae humanae aliud quam nunc est dominium, aliud communionem fuisse.[1] Nam dominium nunc proprium quid significat, quod scilicet ita est alicuius ut alterius non sit eodem modo. Commune autem dicimus, cuius proprietas inter plures consortio

[1] Castrensis on Digest I, 1, 5 (De iustitia et iure, L. Ex hoc iure); Dist. I, C. VII (Ius naturale).

CHAPTER V

Neither the Indian Ocean nor the right of navigation thereon belongs to the Portuguese by title of occupation

If therefore the Portuguese have acquired no legal right over the nations of the East Indies, and their territory and sovereignty, let us consider whether they have been able to obtain exclusive jurisdiction over the sea and its navigation or over trade. Let us first consider the case of the sea.

Now, in the legal phraseology of the Law of Nations, the sea is called indifferently the property of no one (*res nullius*), or a common possession (*res communis*), or public property (*res publica*). It will be most convenient to explain the signification of these terms if we follow the practice of all the poets since Hesiod, of the philosophers and jurists of the past, and distinguish certain epochs, the divisions of which are marked off perhaps not so much by intervals of time as by obvious logic and essential character. And we ought not to be criticised if in our explanation of a law deriving from nature, we use the authority and definition of those whose natural judgment admittedly is held in the highest esteem.

It is therefore necessary to explain that in the earliest stages of human existence both sovereignty and common possession had meanings other than those which they bear at the present time.[1] For nowadays sovereignty means a particular kind of proprietorship, such in fact that it absolutely excludes like possession by any one else. On the other hand, we call a thing 'common' when its ownership

[1] Paul de Castro on Digest I, 1, 5; Dist. I, C. VII.

quodam aut consensu collata est exclusis aliis. Linguarum paupertas coegit voces easdem in re non eadem usurpare. Et sic ista nostri moris nomina ad ius illud pristinum similitudine quadam et imagine referuntur. Commune igitur tunc non aliud fuit quam quod simpliciter proprio opponitur; dominium autem facultas non iniusta utendi re communi, quem usum Scholasticis [1] visum est facti non iuris vocare, quia qui nunc in iure usus vocatur, proprium est quiddam, aut ut illorum more loquar, privative ad alios dicitur.

Iure primo Gentium, quod et Naturale interdum dicitur, et quod poetae alibi aetate aurea, alibi Saturni aut Iustitiae regno depingunt, nihil proprium fuit; quod Cicero dixit: ‘Sunt autem privata nulla natura’. Et Horatius: [2]

Nam PROPRIAE telluris ERVM NATVRA neque illum
Nec me nec quemquam statuit.

Neque enim potuit natura dominos distinguere. Hoc igitur significatu res omnes eo tempore communes fuisse dicimus, idem innuentes quod poetae cum primos homines in medium quaesivisse, et Iustitiam casto foedere res medias tenuisse * dicunt; quod ut clarius explicent, negant eo tempore campos limite partitos, aut commercia fuisse ulla.

. . . . promiscua rura per agros
Praestiterant cunctis COMMVNIA cuncta VIDERI. [3]

[1] Vasquius, Controversiae illustres, c. 1, n. 10; Lib. VI, V, 12, 3 (De verborum significatione, c. Exiit, qui seminat); Clem. V, 11 (De verborum significatione, c. Exivi de paradiso).

[2] Sermones II, 2, 129-130.

[3] Avienus, Aratus 302-303 [promisca quetura V; promiscaque cura A; iura peragros; praestiterat Buhlius, Breyzig].

* [in medium quaerebant, Vergil, Georgica I, 127; medias casto res more tenebas, Avienus, Aratus, 298 (W. P. Mustard)].

or possession is held by several persons jointly according to a kind of partnership or mutual agreement from which all other persons are excluded. Poverty of language compels the use of the same words for things that are not the same. And so because of a certain similarity and likeness, our modern nomenclature is applied to that state of primitive law. Now, in ancient times, 'common' meant simply the opposite of 'particular'; and 'sovereignty' or 'ownership', meant the privilege of lawfully using common property. This seemed to the Scholastics [1] to be a use in fact but not in law, because what now in law is called use, is a particular right, or if I may use their phraseology, is, in respect to other persons, a privative right.

In the primitive law of nations, which is sometimes called Natural Law, and which the poets sometimes portray as having existed in a Golden Age, and sometimes in the reign of Saturn or of Justice, there was no particular right. As Cicero says: 'But nothing is by nature private property'. And Horace: [2] 'For nature has decreed to be the master of private soil neither him, nor me, nor anyone else'. For nature knows no sovereigns. Therefore in this sense we say that in those ancient times all things were held in common, meaning what the poets do when they say that primitive men acquired everything in common, and that Justice maintained a community of goods by means of an inviolable compact. And to make this clearer, they say that in those primitive times the fields were not delimited by boundary lines, and that there was no commercial intercourse. [As Avienus says]: [3] 'The promiscuity of the fields had made everything seem common to all'.

The word 'seemed' is rightly added, owing to the changed meaning of the words, as we have noted above.

[1] Vasquius, Controversiae illustres, c. 1, n. 10; Lib. VI, V, 12, 3; Clem. V, 11.
[2] Satires II, 2, 129-130.
[3] Aratus 302-303.

Recte additum est ' videri ' propter translationem ut diximus vocabuli. Communio autem ista ad usum referebatur: [1]

. . . . pervium cunctis iter,
COMMVNIS VSVS omnium rerum fuit.

Cuius ratione dominium quoddam erat, sed universale, et indefinitum; Deus enim res omnes non huic aut illi dederat, sed humano generi, atque eo modo plures in solidum eiusdem rei domini esse non prohibebantur; quod si hodierna significatione sumamus dominium, contra omnem est rationem. Hoc enim proprietatem includit, quae tunc erat penes neminem. Aptissime autem illud dictum est: [2]

omnia rerum
Vsurpantis erant,

Ad eam vero, quae nunc est, dominiorum distinctionem non impetu quodam, sed paulatim ventum videtur, initium eius monstrante natura. Cum enim res sint nonnullae, quarum usus in abusu consistit, aut quia conversae in substantiam utentis nullum postea usum admittunt, aut quia utendo fiunt ad usum deteriores, in rebus prioris generis, ut cibo et potu, proprietas statim quaedam ab usu non seiuncta emicuit.[3] Hoc enim est proprium esse, ita esse cuiusquam ut et alterius esse non possit; quod deinde ad res posterioris generis, vestes puta, et res mobiles alias aut se moventes ratione quadam productum est.

Quod cum esset, ne res quidem immobiles omnes, agri

[1] Seneca, Octavia 413-414.
[2] Avienus, Aratus 302.
[3] Digest VII, 5 (De usu fructu earum rerum, quae usu consumuntur vel minuuntur); Extravag. XIV, 3 et 5 (De verborum significatione, c. Ad conditorem, et c. Quia quorundam); Thomas Aquinas, Summa II. II, q. 78.

But that kind of common possession relates to use, as is seen from a quotation from Seneca:[1]

> *"Every path was free,*
> *All things were used in common."*

According to his reasoning there was a kind of sovereignty, but it was universal and unlimited. For God had not given all things to this individual or to that, but to the entire human race, and thus a number of persons, as it were *en masse,* were not debarred from being substantially sovereigns or owners of the same thing, which is quite contradictory to our modern meaning of sovereignty. For it now implies particular or private ownership, a thing which no one then had. Avienus has said very pertinently:[2] 'All things belonged to him who had possession of them'.

It seems certain that the transition to the present distinction of ownerships did not come violently, but gradually, nature herself pointing out the way. For since there are some things, the use of which consists in their being used up, either because having become part of the very substance of the user they can never be used again, or because by use they become less fit for future use, it has become apparent, especially in dealing with the first category, such things as food and drink for example, that a certain kind of ownership is inseparable from use.[3] For 'own' implies that a thing belongs to some one person, in such a way that it cannot belong to any other person. By the process of reasoning this was next extended to things of the second category, such as clothes and movables and some living things.

When that had come about, not even immovables, such,

[1] Octavia 413-414 [Translation by E. I. Harris (Act II, Scene 1)].

[2] Aratus 302.

[3] Digest VII, 5; Extravagantes of Pope John XXII, XIV, 3 and 5; Thomas Aquinas, Summa II. II, q. 78.

puta, indivisae manere potuerunt; quamquam enim horum usus non simpliciter in abusu consistat, eorum tamen usus abusus cuiusdam causa comparatus est, ut arva et arbusta cibi causa, pascua etiam vestium; omnium autem usibus promiscue sufficere non possunt. Repertae proprietati lex posita est, quae naturam imitaretur. Sicut enim initio per applicationem corporalem usus ille habebatur, unde proprietatem primum ortam diximus, ita simili applicatione res proprias cuiusque fieri placuit. Haec est quae dicitur occupatio, voce accommodatissima ad eas res quae ante in medio positae fuerant; quo Seneca Tragicus alludit: [1]

IN MEDIO est scelus
POSITVM OCCVPANTI.

Et Philosophus: [2] ' Equestria OMNIVM equitum Romanorum sunt. In illis tamen locus meus fit PROPRIVS, quem OCCVPAVI '. Hinc Quintilianus dicit,[3] quod omnibus nascitur, industriae esse praemium; et Tullius,[4] factas esse veteri occupatione res eorum qui quondam in vacua venerant.

Occupatio autem haec in his rebus quae possessioni renituntur, ut sunt ferae bestiae, perpetua esse debet, in aliis sufficit, corpore coeptam possessionem animo retineri. Occupatio in mobilibus est apprehensio, in immobilibus

[1] Thyestes 203-204 (F. CXXII).
[2] De beneficiis VII, 12, 3.
[3] Ps. Quintilianus, Declamatio XIII (Pro paupere).
[4] Cicero, De officiis I.

for instance, as fields, could remain unapportioned. For although their use does not consist merely in consumption, nevertheless it is bound up with subsequent consumption, as fields and plants are used to get food, and pastures to get clothing. There is, however, not enough fixed property to satisfy the use of everybody indiscriminately.

When property or ownership was invented, the law of property was established to imitate nature. For as that use began in connection with bodily needs, from which as we have said property first arose, so by a similar connection it was decided that things were the property of individuals. This is called 'occupation', a word most appropriate to those things which in former times had been held in common. It is this to which Seneca alludes in his tragedy Thyestes,

"Crime is between us to be seized by one."[1]

And in one of his philosophical writings he also says:[2] 'The equestrian rows of seats belong to all the equites; nevertheless, the seat of which I have taken possession is my own private place'. Further, Quintilian remarks[3] that a thing which is created for all is the reward of industry, and Cicero says[4] that things which have been occupied for a long time become the property of those who originally found them unoccupied.

This occupation or possession, however, in the case of things which resist seizure, like wild animals for example, must be uninterrupted or perpetually maintained, but in the case of other things it is sufficient if after physical possession is once taken the intention to possess is maintained. Possession of movables implies seizure, and possession of

[1] 203-204 [E. I. Harris' translation (Act II, Scene 1)].
[2] De beneficiis VII, 12, 3.
[3] Speech XIII, In behalf of the poor man.
[4] De officiis I.

instructio aut limitatio; unde Hermogenianus cum dominia distincta dicit, addit, agris terminos positos, aedificia collocata.[1] Hic rerum status a poetis indicatur:

Tum laqueis captare feras, et fallere visco
Inventum.

Tum primum subiere domos.[2]

COMMVNEMQVE PRIVS, ceu lumina solis et auras
Cautus humum longo signavit LIMITE mensor.[3]

Celebratur post haec, ut Hermogenianus indicat, commercium cuius gratia

Fluctibus ignotis insultavere carinae.[4]

Eodem autem tempore et respublicae institui coeperunt. Atque ita earum quae a prima communione divulsa erant duo facta sunt genera. Alia enim sunt publica, hoc est, populi propria (quae est genuina istius vocis significatio) alia mere privata, hoc est, singulorum. Occupatio autem publica eodem modo fit, quo privata. Seneca:[5] 'Fines Atheniensium, aut Campanorum vocamus, quos deinde inter se vicini privata terminatione distinguunt'. Gens enim unaquaeque

[1] Digest I, 1, 5 (De iustitia et iure, L. Ex hoc iure).
[2] Vergil, Georgica I, 139-140; Ovid, Metamorphoses I, 121.
[3] Ovid, Metamorphoses I, 135-136.
[4] Ovid, Metamorphoses I, 134 (exsultavere, Magnus).
[5] De beneficiis VII, 4, 3.

immovables either the erection of buildings or some determination of boundaries, such as fencing in. Hence Hermogenianus, in speaking of separate ownerships, adds the boundaries set to the fields and the buildings thereon constructed.[1] This state of things is described thus by the poets Vergil and Ovid:

> "*Then toils for beasts, and lime for birds, were found,*"[2]
>
> *Then first men made homes.*
>
> "*Then landmarks limited to each his right,*
> *For all before was common as the light.*"[3]

In still another place, as Hermogenianus points out, Ovid praises commerce, for the sake of which:[4]

> '*Ships in triumph sail the unknown seas*'.

At the same time, however, states began to be established, and so two categories were made of the things which had been wrested away from early ownership in common. For some things were public, that is, were the property of the people (which is the real meaning of that expression), while other things were private, that is, were the property of individuals. Ownership, however, both public and private, arises in the same way. On this point Seneca says:[5] 'We speak in general of the land of the Athenians or the Campanians. It is the same land which again by means of private boundaries is divided among individual owners'.

[1] Digest I, 1, 5.

[2] Vergil, Georgics I, 139-140 [Dryden's translation I, 211]; Ovid, Metamorphoses I, 121.

[3] Ovid, Metamorphoses I, 135-136 [Dryden's translation I (English Poets XX, 432)].

[4] Ovid, Metamorphoses I, 134.

[5] De beneficiis VII, 4, 3.

> *PARTITA FINES regna constituit, novas*
> *Extruxit VRBES.*[1]

Hoc modo dicit Cicero agrum Arpinatem Arpinatium dici, Tusculanum Tusculanorum: 'similisque est', inquit, 'privatarum possessionum discriptio. Ex quo quia suum cuiusque fit eorum, quae natura fuerant COMMVNIA, quod cuique obtigit, id quisque teneat'.[2] Contra autem Thucydides[3] eam terram quae in divisione populo nulli obvenit, *ἀόριστον*, hoc est, indefinitam, et limitibus nullis circumscriptam vocat.[4]

Ex his quae hactenus dicta sunt duo intelligi possunt. Prius est, eas res quae occupari non possunt, aut occupatae numquam sunt, nullius proprias esse posse; quia omnis proprietas ab occupatione coeperit. Alterum vero, eas res omnes, quae ita a natura comparatae sunt, ut aliquo utente nihilominus aliis quibusvis ad usum promiscue sufficiant, eius hodieque condicionis esse, et perpetuo esse debere cuius fuerant cum primum a natura proditae sunt. Hoc Cicero voluit:[5] 'Ac latissime quidem patens hominibus inter ipsos, omnibus inter omnes societas haec est; in qua omnium rerum, quas ad communem hominum usum natura genuit, est servanda communitas'. Sunt autem omnes res huius generis, in quibus sine detrimento alterius alteri commodari potest. Hinc illud esse dicit Cicero:[6] 'Non prohibere aqua profluente'. Nam aqua profluens qua talis non qua flumen

[1] Octavia 431-432.
[2] De officiis I, 21.
[3] Thucydides I, 139, 2.
[4] Duarenus on Digest I, 8 (De divisione rerum).
[5] De officiis I, 51.
[6] De officiis I, 52.

'For each nation', Seneca says in another place, 'made its territories into separate kingdoms and built new cities'.[1] Thus Cicero says: "On this principle the lands of Arpinum are said to belong to the Arpinates, the Tusculan lands to the Tusculans; and similar is the assignment of private property. Therefore, inasmuch as in each case some of those things which by nature had been common property became the property of individuals, each one should retain possession of that which has fallen to his lot."[2] On the other hand Thucydides[3] calls the land which in the division falls to no nation, *ἀόριστος*, that is, undefined, and undetermined by boundaries.[4]

Two conclusions may be drawn from what has thus far been said. The first is, that that which cannot be occupied, or which never has been occupied, cannot be the property of any one, because all property has arisen from occupation. The second is, that all that which has been so constituted by nature that although serving some one person it still suffices for the common use of all other persons, is today and ought in perpetuity to remain in the same condition as when it was first created by nature. This is what Cicero meant when he wrote: "This then is the most comprehensive bond that unites together men as men and all to all; and under it the common right to all things that nature has produced for the common use of man is to be maintained."[5] All things which can be used without loss to any one else come under this category. Hence, says Cicero, comes the well known prohibition:[6] 'Deny no one the water that flows by'. For running water considered as such and not as a

[1] Octavia 431-432 [Grotius here takes a slight liberty with the context].
[2] De officiis I, 21 [Walter Miller's (Loeb) translation, page 23].
[3] History I, 139, 2.
[4] Duaren [a French humanist (1509-1559)], on Digest I, 8.
[5] De officiis I, 51 [Walter Miller's (Loeb) translation, page 55].
[6] De officiis I, 52.

est, inter communia omnium a Iurisconsultis refertur: et a Poeta:[1]

Quid prohibetis AQVAS? VSVS COMMVNIS aquarum est.
Nec solem PROPRIVM NATVRA nec AERA fecit,
Nec tenues VNDAS: in PVBLICA munera veni.

Dicit haec non esse natura propria, sicut Vlpianus[2] natura omnibus patere, tum quia primum a natura prodita sunt, et in nullius adhuc dominium pervenerunt (ut loquitur Neratius[3]); tum quia ut Cicero dicit, a natura ad usum communem genita videntur. Publica autem vocat tralatitia significatione, non quae ad populum aliquem, sed quae ad societatem humanam pertinent, quae publica Iuris gentium in Legibus vocantur, hoc est, communia omnium, propria nullius.

Huius generis est Aër, duplici ratione, tum quia occupari non potest, tum quia usum promiscuum hominibus debet. Et eisdem de causis commune est omnium Maris Elementum, infinitum scilicet ita, ut possideri non queat, et omnium usibus accommodatum: sive navigationem respicimus, sive etiam piscaturam. Cuius autem iuris est mare, eiusdem sunt si qua mare aliis usibus eripiendo sua fecit, ut arenae maris, quarum pars terris continua litus dicitur.[4] Recte igitur Cicero:[5] 'quid tam COMMVNE quam Mare fluc-

[1] Ovid, Metamorphoses VI, 349-351 (aquis, 349, and ad publica, 351, Merkel).

[2] Digest VIII, 4, 13 (Communia praediorum, L. Venditor).

[3] Digest XLI, 1, 14 (De adquirendo rerum dominio, L. Quod in litore); Comines, Memoirs III, 2; Donellus IV, 2; Digest XLI, 3, 49 (De usucapionibus).

[4] Digest I, 8, 10 (De divisione rerum, L. Aristo).

[5] Cicero, Loco citato. [Pro Sex. Roscio Amerino 26, 72].

stream, is classed by the jurists among the things common to all mankind; as is done also by Ovid:[1] ' Why do you deny me water? Its use is free to all. Nature has made neither sun nor air nor waves private property; they are public gifts '.

He says that these things are not by nature private possession, but that, as Ulpian claims,[2] they are by nature things open to the use of all, both because in the first place they were produced by nature, and have never yet come under the sovereignty of any one, as Neratius says;[3] and in the second place because, as Cicero says, they seem to have been created by nature for common use. But the poet uses ' public ', in its usual meaning, not of those things which belong to any one people, but to human society as a whole; that is to say, things which are called ' public ' are, according to the Laws of the law of nations, the common property of all, and the private property of none.

The air belongs to this class of things for two reasons. First, it is not susceptible of occupation; and second its common use is destined for all men. For the same reasons the sea is common to all, because it is so limitless that it cannot become a possession of any one, and because it is adapted for the use of all, whether we consider it from the point of view of navigation or of fisheries. Now, the same right which applies to the sea applies also to the things which the sea has carried away from other uses and made its own, such for example as the sands of the sea, of which the portion adjoining the land is called the coast or shore.[4] Cicero therefore argues correctly:[5] ' What is so common as

[1] Metamorphoses VI, 349-351.

[2] Digest VIII, 4, 13.

[3] Digest XLI, 1, 14; Comines, Memoirs III, 2; Donellus IV, 2; Digest XLI, 3, 49. [Philippe de Comines (1445-1509), a French historian, and one of the negotiators of the treaty of Senlis (1493).]

[4] Digest I, 8, 10.

[5] Pro Sex. Roscio Amerino 26, 72.

tuantibus, LITVS eiectis '? Etiam Vergilius auram, undam, litus cunctis patere dicit.

Haec igitur sunt illa quae Romani vocant communia omnium iure naturali [1] aut quod idem esse diximus, publica iurisgentium, sicut et usum eorum modo communem, modo publicum vocant. Quamquam vero etiam ea nullius esse, quod ad proprietatem attinet, recte dicantur, multum tamen differunt ab his quae nullius sunt, et communi usui attributa non sunt, ut ferae, pisces, aves; nam ista si quis occupet, in ius proprium transire possunt, illa vero totius humanitatis consensu proprietati in perpetuum excepta sunt propter usum, qui cum sit omnium, non magis omnibus ab uno eripi potest, quam a te mihi quod meum est. Hoc est quod Cicero dicit inter prima esse Iustitiae munera, rebus communibus pro communibus uti. Scholastici dicerent esse communia alia affirmative, alia privative. Distinctio haec non modo Iurisprudentibus usitata est, sed vulgi etiam confessionem exprimit; unde apud Athenaeum convivator mare commune esse dicit, at pisces capientium fieri. Et in Plautina Rudente servo dicenti,[2] ' Mare quidem commune certost omnibus', assentit piscator, addenti autem, ' In mari inventust communi ' recte occurrit:

> *Meum quod rete atque hami nancti sunt, meum*
> *potissimumst.*

[1] Institutes II, 1, 1 et 5 (De rerum divisione, § Et quidem naturali; § Litorum); Digest I, 8, 1, 2, 10 (De rerum divisione); Digest XLI, 1, 14 et 50 (De adquirendo rerum dominio, L. Quod in litore, et L. Quamvis); Digest XLVII, 10, 13 (De iniuriis, L. Iniuriarum § si quis me); Digest XLIII, 8, 3 (Ne quid in loco publico, L. Litora) et 4-7.

[2] 975, 977, 985 (IV, 3).

the sea for those who are being tossed upon it, the shore for those who have been cast thereon'. Vergil also says that the air, the sea, and the shore are open to all men.

These things therefore are what the Romans call 'common' to all men by natural law,[1] or as we have said, 'public' according to the law of nations; and indeed they call their use sometimes common, sometimes public. Nevertheless, although those things are with reason said to be *res nullius*, so far as private ownership is concerned, still they differ very much from those things which, though also *res nullius*, have not been marked out for common use, such for example as wild animals, fish, and birds. For if any one seizes those things and assumes possession of them, they can become objects of private ownership, but the things in the former category by the consensus of opinion of all mankind are forever exempt from such private ownership on account of their susceptibility to universal use; and as they belong to all they cannot be taken away from all by any one person any more than what is mine can be taken away from me by you. And Cicero says that one of the first gifts of Justice is the use of common property for common benefit. The Scholastics would define one of these categories as common in an affirmative, the other in a privative sense. This distinction is not only familiar to jurists, but it also expresses the popular belief. In Athenaeus for instance the host is made to say that the sea is the common property of all, but that fish are the private property of him who catches them. And in Plautus' Rudens when the slave says:[2] 'The sea is certainly common to all persons', the fisherman agrees; but when the slave adds: 'Then what is found in the common sea is common property', he rightly objects, saying: 'But what my net and hooks have taken, is absolutely my own'.

[1] Institutes II, 1, 1 and 5; Digest I, 8, 1, 2, 10; XLI, 1, 14 and 50; XLVII, 10, 13; XLIII, 8, 3, and 4-7.

[2] Act IV, Scene 3 (975, 977, 985).

Mare igitur proprium omnino alicuius fieri non potest, quia natura commune hoc esse non permittit, sed iubet, immo ne litus quidem;[1] nisi quod haec addenda est interpretatio; ut si quid earum rerum per naturam occupari possit, id eatenus occupantis fiat, quatenus ea occupatione usus ille promiscuus non laeditur. Quod merito receptum est; nam cum ita se habet, cessat utraque exceptio per quam evenisse diximus, ne omnia in eius proprium transcriberentur.

Quoniam igitur inaedificatio species est occupationis, in litore licet aedificare, si id fieri potest sine ceterorum incommodo,[2] ut Pomponius loquitur, quod ex Scaevola explicabimus, nisi usus publicus, hoc est communis impediretur. Et qui aedificaverit, soli dominus fiet, quia id solum nec ullius proprium, nec ad usum communem necessarium fuit. Est igitur occupantis; sed non diutius quam durat occupatio, quia reluctari mare possessioni videtur, exemplo ferae, quae si in naturalem se libertatem receperit, non ultra captoris est, ita et litus postliminio mari cedit.

Quicquid autem privatum fieri occupando, idem et publicum, hoc est populi proprium posse ostendimus.[3] Sic litus Imperi Romani finibus inclusum, populi Romani esse Celsus

[1] Donellus IV, 2.

[2] Digest XXXIX, 2, 24 (De damno infecto, L. Fluminum); other references same as note 1, page 29.

[3] Donellus IV, 2 et 9; also references in note 1, page 29.

Therefore the sea can in no way become the private property of any one, because nature not only allows but enjoins its common use.[1] Neither can the shore become the private property of any one. The following qualification, however, must be made. If any part of these things is by nature susceptible of occupation, it may become the property of the one who occupies it only so far as such occupation does not affect its common use. This qualification is deservedly recognized. For in such a case both conditions vanish through which it might eventuate, as we have said, that all of it would pass into private ownership.

Since therefore, to cite Pomponius, building is one kind of occupation, it is permissible to build upon the shore, if this can be done without inconvenience to other people;[2] that is to say (I here follow Scaevola) if such building can be done without hindrance to public or common use of the shore. And whoever shall have constructed a building under the aforesaid circumstances will become the owner of the ground upon which said building is; because this ground is neither the property of any one else, nor is it necessary to common use. It becomes therefore the property of the occupier, but his ownership lasts no longer than his occupation lasts, inasmuch as the sea seems by nature to resist ownership. For just as a wild animal, if it shall have escaped and thus recovered its natural liberty, is no longer the property of its captor, so also the sea may recover its possession of the shore.

We have now shown that whatever by occupation can become private property can also become public property, that is, the private property of a whole nation.[3] And so Celsus considered the shore included within the limits of the Roman Empire to be the property of the Roman people.

[1] Donellus IV, 2.

[2] Digest XXXIX, 2, 24; other references same as note 1, page 29.

[3] Donellus IV, 2 and 9; also references in note 1, page 29.

existimat; quod si ita est, minime mirandum est, eundem Populum subditis suis occupandi litoris modum per Principem aut Praetorem potuisse concedere. Ceterum et haec occupatio non minus quam privata ita restringenda est, ne ulterius porrigatur, quam ut salvus sit usus Iurisgentium. Nemo igitur potest a Populo Romano [1] ad litus maris accedere prohiberi, et retia siccare, et alia facere, quae semel omnes homines in perpetuum sibi licere voluerunt.

Maris autem natura hoc differt a litore, quod mare nisi exigua sui parte nec inaedificari facile, nec includi potest; et ut posset, hoc ipsum tamen vix contingeret, sine usus promiscui impedimento. Si quid tamen exiguum ita occupari potest, id occupanti conceditur. Hyperbole est igitur [2]

Contracta pisces aequora sentiunt
Iactis in altum molibus.

Nam Celsus iactas in mare pilas eius esse dicit qui iecerit.[3] Sed id non concedendum si deterior maris usus eo modo futurus sit. Et Vlpianus eum qui molem in mare iacit, ita tuendum dicit si nemo damnum sentiat. Nam si cui haec res nocitura sit, interdictum utique, 'Ne quid in loco publico fiat' competiturum. Vt et Labeo, si quid tale in mare struatur, interdictum vult competere, 'Ne quid in mari, quo portus, statio, iterve navigiis deterius sit, fiat'. [4]

[1] Digest I, 8, 4 (De divisione rerum, L. Nemo igitur); XLIII, 8, 3 (Ne quid in loco publico, L. Litora).

[2] Horace, Carmina III, i, 33-34.

[3] Digest XLIII, 8, 3 (as in note 1); 8, 2 (eod. tit., L. Praetor, § Adversus).

[4] Digest XLIII, 12, 1 (De fluminibus, L. Ait praetor, § Si in mari).

There is not therefore the least reason for surprise that the Roman people through their emperors or praetors was able to grant to its subjects the right of occupying the shore. This public occupation, however, no less than private occupation, was subject to the restriction that it should not infringe on international rights. Therefore the Roman people could not forbid any one from having access to the seashore,[1] and from spreading his fishing nets there to dry, and from doing other things which all men long ago decided were always permissible.

The nature of the sea, however, differs from that of the shore, because the sea, except for a very restricted space, can neither easily be built upon, nor inclosed; if the contrary were true yet this could hardly happen without hindrance to the general use. Nevertheless, if any small portion of the sea can be thus occupied, the occupation is recognized. The famous hyperbole of Horace must be quoted here: " The fishes note the narrowing of the waters by piers of rock laid in their depths." [2]

Now Celsus holds that piles driven into the sea belong to the man who drove them.[3] But such an act is not permissible if the use of the sea be thereby impaired. And Ulpian says that whoever builds a breakwater must be protected if it is not prejudicial to the interests of any one; for if this construction is likely to work an injury to any one, the injunction 'Nothing may be built on public property' would apply. Labeo, however, holds that in case any such construction should be made in the sea, the following injunction is to be enforced: 'Nothing may be built in the sea whereby the harbor, the roadstead, or the channel be rendered less safe for navigation'.[4]

[1] Digest I, 8, 4; XLIII, 8, 3.
[2] Odes III, i, 33-34 [Bennett's (Loeb) translation, page 171].
[3] Digest XLIII, 8, 3; 8, 2.
[4] Digest XLIII, 12, 1.

Quae autem navigationis eadem piscatus habenda est ratio, ut communis maneat omnibus. Neque tamen peccabit si quis in maris diverticulo piscandi locum sibi palis circumsepiat, atque ita privatum faciat; sicut Lucullus exciso apud Neapolim monte ad villam suam maria admisit.[1] Et huius generis, puto fuisse piscinas maritimas quarum Varro et Columella meminerunt. Nec Martialis alio spectavit, cum de Formiano Apollinaris loquitur: [2]

Si quando NEREVS sentit Aeoli regnum,
Ridet procellas tuta de SVO mensa.

Et Ambrosius: [3] 'Inducis mare intra praedia tua ne desint belluae'. Hinc apparere potest quae mens Pauli fuerit, cum dicit,[4] si maris proprium ius ad aliquem pertineat, *uti possidetis* interdictum ei competere. Esse quidem hoc interdictum ad privatas causas comparatum, non autem ad publicas, (in quibus etiam ea comprehenduntur quae iure gentium communi facere possumus) sed hic iam agi de iure fruendo quod ex causa privata contingat, non publica, sive communi. Nam teste Marciano, quicquid occupatum est et occupari potuit,[5] id iam non est iurisgentium, sicut est mare. Exempli causa, si quis Lucullum aut Apollinarem in privato suo, quatenus diverticulum maris incluserant, piscari prohibuisset, dandum illis inter-

[1] Pliny, Naturalis historia IX, 54, 170.
[2] Martial, Epigrammata X, 30, 19-20.
[3] De Nabuthe, cap. 3.
[4] Digest XLVII, 10, 14 (De iniuriis, L. Sane si maris).
[5] Cf. note 1, page 31.

Now the same principle which applies to navigation applies also to fishing, namely, that it remains free and open to all. Nevertheless there shall be no prejudice if any one shall by fencing off with stakes an inlet of the sea make a fish pond for himself, and so establish a private preserve. Thus Lucullus once brought the water of the sea to his villa by cutting a tunnel through a mountain near Naples.[1] I suspect too that the seawater reservoirs for fish mentioned by Varro and Columella were of this sort. And Martial had the same thing in mind when he says of the Formian villa of Apollinaris:[2] 'Whenever Nereus feels the power of Aeolus, the table safe in its own resources laughs at the gale'. Ambrose also has something to say on the same subject:[3] 'You bring the very sea into your estates that you may not lack for fish'. In the light of all this the meaning of Paulus is clear when he says[4] that if any one has a private right over the sea, the rule *uti possidetis* applies. This rule however is applicable only to private suits, and not to public ones, among which are also to be included those suits which can be brought under the common law of nations. But here the question is one which concerns the right of use arising in a private suit, but not in a public or common one. For according to the authority of Marcianus whatever has been occupied and can be occupied[5] is no longer subject to the law of nations as the sea is. Let us take an example. If any one had prevented Lucullus or Apollinaris from fishing in the private fish ponds which they had made by inclosing a small portion of the sea, according to the opinion of Paulus they would have the right of bringing

[1] Pliny, Natural History IX, 54, 170.
[2] Epigrams X, 30, 19-20.
[3] De Nabuthe, cap. 3.
[4] Digest XLVII, 10, 14.
[5] See note 1, page 31.

dictum Paulus putavit non solum iniuriarum actionem, ob causam scilicet privatae possessionis.[1]

Immo in diverticulo maris, sicut in diverticulo fluminis, si locum talem occuparim, ibique piscatus sim, maxime si animum privatim possidendi plurium annorum continuatione testatus fuerim, alterum eodem iure uti prohibebo; ut ex Marciano colligimus, non aliter quam in lacu qui mei dominii est. Quod verum quam diu durat occupatio, quemadmodum in litore antea diximus. Extra diverticulum idem non erit, ne scilicet communis usus impediatur.[2]

Ante aedes igitur meas aut praetorium ut piscari aliquem prohibeant usurpatum quidem est, sed nullo iure, adeo quidem ut Vlpianus contempta ea usurpatione si quis prohibeatur iniuriarum dicat agi posse.[3] Hoc Imperator Leo (cuius Legibus non utimur) contra iuris rationem mutavit, voluitque *πρόθυρα,* hoc est, vestibula maritima eorum esse propria, qui oram habitarent, ibique eos ius piscandi habere;[4] quod tamen ita procedere voluit, ut septis quibusdam remoratoriis quas *ἐποχάς* Graeci vocant, locus ille occuparetur; existimans nimirum non fore ut quis exiguam maris portionem alteri invideret qui ipse toto mari ad piscandum admitteretur. Certe ut quis magnam maris partem, etiam si possit, publicis utilitatibus eripiat, non tolerandae est improbitatis, in quam merito Vir Sanctus invehitur:[5]

[1] Digest XLIV, 3, 7 (De diversis, L. Si quisquam).
[2] Digest XLI, 3, 45 (De usucapionibus, L. Praescriptio).
[3] Digest XLVII, 10, 13 (De iniuriis, L. Iniuriarum, § Si quis me).
[4] Novella Leonis, 102, 103, 104; cf. Cuiacium XIV, 1.
[5] Hexameron V, 10, 27.

an injunction, not merely an action for damages based on private ownership.[1]

Indeed, if I shall have staked off such an inclosure in an inlet of the sea, just as in a branch of a river, and have fished there, especially if by doing so continuously for many years I shall have given proof of my intention to establish private ownership, I shall certainly prevent any one else from enjoying the same rights. I gather from Marcianus that this case is identical with that of the ownership of a lake, and it is true however long occupation lasts, as we have said above about the shore. But outside of an inlet this will not hold, for then the common use of the sea might be hindered.[2]

Therefore if any one is prevented from fishing in front of my town house or country seat, it is a usurpation, but an illegal one, although Ulpian, who rather makes light of this usurpation, does say that if any one is so prevented he can bring an action for damages.[3] The Emperor Leo, whose laws we do not use, contrary to the intent of the law, changed this, and declared that the entrances, or vestibules as it were, to the sea, were the private property of those who inhabited the shore, and that they had the right of fishing there.[4] However he attached this condition, that the place should be occupied by certain jetty or pile constructions, such as the Greeks call *ἐποχαί*, thinking doubtless that no one who was himself allowed to fish anywhere in the sea would grudge any one else a small portion of it. To be sure it would be an intolerable outrage for any one to snatch away, even if he could do so, from public use a large area of the sea; an act which is justly reprehended by the Holy Man,[5] who says: 'The lords of the earth claim for

[1] Digest XLIV, 3, 7.

[2] Digest XLI, 3, 45.

[3] Digest XLVII, 10, 13.

[4] Novels of Leo, 102, 103, 104; See also Cujas XIV, 1.

[5] Hexameron V, 10, 27 [St. Ambrose (c. 333-397), Bishop of Milan, is meant].

'SPATIA MARIS sibi vindicant IVRE MANCIPII, pisciumque iura sicut vernaculorum conditione sibi servitii subiecta commemorant. Iste, inquit, SINVS maris meus est; ille alterius. Dividunt elementa sibi potentes'.

Est igitur Mare in numero earum rerum quae in commercio non sunt,[1] hoc est, quae proprii iuris fieri non possunt. Vnde sequitur si proprie loquamur, nullam Maris partem in territorio populi alicuius posse censeri. Quod ipsum Placentinus sensisse videtur, cum dixit: Mare ita esse commune, ut in nullius dominio sit nisi solius Dei; et Ioannes Faber, cum mare asserit relictum in suo iure, et esse primaevo, quo omnia erant communia.[2] Alioquin nihil differrent quae sunt omnium communia ab his quae publica proprie dicuntur, ut mare a flumine. Flumen populus occupare potuit, ut inclusum finibus suis, mare non potuit.

Territoria autem sunt ex occupationibus populorum, ut privata dominia ex occupationibus singulorum. Vidit hoc Celsus, qui clare satis distinguit inter litora,[3] quae Populus Romanus occupare potuit, ita tamen ut usui communi non noceretur, et mare quod pristinam naturam retinuit. Nec ulla lex diversum indicat.[4] Quae vero leges a contrariae

[1] Donellus IV, 6.

[2] Joannes Faber on Institutes II, 1 (§ Litorum); Digest XIV, 2, 9 (De Lege Rhodia, L. 'Αξίωσις).

[3] Digest XLIII, 8, 3 (Ne quid in loco publico, L. Litora).

[4] Digest V, 1, 9 (De iudiciis, L. Insulae); XXXIX, 4, 15 (De publicanis, L. Caesar); Gloss. on Digest I, 8, 2 (De divisione rerum, L. Quaedam); Institutes II, 1; Baldus on Quaedam (above).

themselves a wide expanse of sea by *jus mancipii,* and they regard the right of fishing as a servitude over which their right is the same as that over their slaves. That gulf, says one, belongs to me, and that gulf to some one else. They divide the very elements among themselves, these great men '!

Therefore the sea is one of those things which is not an article of merchandise,[1] and which cannot become private property. Hence it follows, to speak strictly, that no part of the sea can be considered as the territory of any people whatsoever. Placentinus seems to have recognized this when he said: ' The sea is a thing so clearly common to all, that it cannot be the property of any one save God alone '. Johannes Faber [2] also asserts that the sea has been left *sui juris,* and remains in the primitive condition where all things were common. If it were otherwise there would be no difference between the things which are ' common to all ', and those which are strictly termed ' public '; no difference, that is, between the sea and a river. A nation can take possession of a river, as it is inclosed within their boundaries, with the sea, they cannot do so.

Now, public territory arises out of the occupation of nations, just as private property arises out of the occupation of individuals. This is recognized by Celsus, who has drawn a sharp distinction between the shores of the sea,[3] which the Roman people could occupy in such a way that its common use was not harmed, and the sea itself, which retained its primitive nature. In fact no law intimates a contrary view.[4] Such laws as are cited by writers who are of

[1] Donellus IV, 6.

[2] On Institutes II, 1; Digest XIV, 2, 9 [Johannes Faber (c. 1570-c. 1640) was Bishop of Vienna, and Court preacher to Emperor Ferdinand. He was known popularly as ' Malleus Haereticorum '].

[3] Digest XLIII, 8, 3.

[4] Digest V, 1, 9; XXXIX, 4, 15; Glossators on Digest I, 8, 2; Institutes II, 1; Baldus on L. Quaedam, in Digest I, 8, 2.

sententiae auctoribus citantur, aut de insulis loquuntur, quas clarum est occupari potuisse, aut de portu qui non communis est, sed proprie publicus.

Qui vero dicunt mare aliquod esse Imperi Romani, dictum suum ita interpretantur, ut dicant ius illud in mare ultra protectionem et iurisdictionem non procedere; quod illi ius a proprietate distinguunt; nec forte satis animadvertunt idipsum quod Populus Romanus classes praesidio navigantium disponere potuit, et deprehensos in mari piratas punire, non ex proprio, sed ex communi iure accidisse, quod et aliae liberae gentes in mari habent. Illud interim fatemur, potuisse inter gentes aliquas convenire, ut capti in maris hac vel illa parte, huius aut illius reipublicae iudicium subirent, atque ita ad commoditatem distinguendae iurisdictionis in mari fines describi, quod ipsos quidem eam sibi legem ferentes obligat,[1] at alios populos non item; neque locum alicuius proprium facit, sed in personas contrahentium ius constituit.

Quae distinctio ut naturali rationi consentanea est, ita Vlpiani responso quodam comprobatur, qui rogatus an duorum praediorum maritimorum dominus, alteri eorum quod venderet servitutem potuisset imponere, ne inde in certo maris loco piscari liceret, respondet: rem quidem ipsam, mare scilicet, servitute nulla affici potuisse, quia per naturam hoc omnibus pateret, sed cum bona fides contractus legem venditionis servari exposceret, personas possidentium et in ius eorum succedentium per istam legem obligari.

[1] Baldus, Quibus modis feudi amittuntur, c. In principio, 2 col.; Code XI, 13, 1; Angelus on Digest XLVII, 10, 14 (De iniuriis, L. Sane); Digest VIII, 4, 13 (Communia praediorum, L. Venditor fundi) et 4 (L. Caveri).

the contrary opinion apply either to islands, which evidently could be occupied, or to harbors, which are not 'common', but 'public', that is, 'national'.

Now those who say that a certain sea belonged to the Roman people explain their statement to mean that the right of the Romans did not extend beyond protection and jurisdiction; this right they distinguish from ownership. Perchance they do not pay sufficient attention to the fact that although the Roman People were able to maintain fleets for the protection of navigation and to punish pirates captured on the sea, it was not done by private right, but by the common right which other free peoples also enjoy on the sea. We recognize, however, that certain peoples have agreed that pirates captured in this or in that part of the sea should come under the jurisdiction of this state or of that, and further that certain convenient limits of distinct jurisdiction have been apportioned on the sea. Now, this agreement does bind those who are parties to it,[1] but it has no binding force on other nations, nor does it make the delimited area of the sea the private property of any one. It merely constitutes a personal right between contracting parties.

This distinction so conformable to natural reason is also confirmed by a reply once made by Ulpian. Upon being asked whether the owner of two maritime estates could on selling either of them impose on it such a servitude as the prohibition of fishing in a particular part of the sea, he replied that the thing in question, evidently the sea, could not be subjected to a servitude, because it was by nature open to all persons; but that since a contract made in good faith demands that the condition of a sale be respected, the present possessors and those who succeed to

[1] Baldus, Quibus modis feudi amittuntur, chapter beginning In principio, second column; Code XI, 13, 1; Angeli on Digest XLVII, 10, 14; Digest VIII, 4, 13 and 4.

Verum est loqui Iurisconsultum de praediis privatis, et lege privata, sed in territorio et lege populorum eadem hic est ratio, quia populi respectu totius generis humani privatorum locum obtinent.

Similiter reditus qui in piscationes maritimas constituti Regalium numero censentur, non rem, hoc est mare, aut piscationem, sed personas obligant.[1] Quare subditi, in quos legem ferendi potestas Reipublicae aut Principi ex consensu competit, ad onera ista compelli forte poterunt; sed exteris ius piscandi ubique immune esse debet, ne servitus imponatur mari quod servire non potest.

Non enim maris eadem quae fluminis ratio est:[2] quod cum sit publicum, id est populi, ius etiam in eo piscandi a populo aut principe concedi aut locari potest, ita ut ei qui conduxit, etiam interdictum Veteres dederint, de loco publico fruendo, addita condicione si is cui locandi ius fuerit, fruendum alicui locaverit;[3] quae condicio in mari evenire non potest. Ceterum qui ipsam piscationem numerant inter Regalia, ne quidem illum locum quem interpretabantur satis inspexerunt, quod Iserniam et Alvotum non latuit.

Demonstratum est[4] nec populo nec privato cuipiam ius

[1] C. Quae sint Regalia, in Feudis.

[2] Balbus, De praescriptionibus IV, 5; 1, q. 6, n. 4.

[3] Digest XLVII, 10, 13 (De iniuriis, L. Iniuriarum, § 7, v. conductori); XLIII, 9, 1 (De loco publico fruendo).

[4] Cf. note 1.

their rights were bound to observe that condition. It is true that the jurist is speaking of private estates and of private law, but in speaking here of the territory of peoples and of public law the same reasoning applies, because from the point of view of the whole human race peoples are treated as individuals.

Similarly, revenues levied on maritime fisheries are held to belong to the Crown, but they do not bind the sea itself or the fisheries, but only the persons engaged in fishing.[1] Wherefore subjects, for whom a state or a ruler is by common consent competent to make laws, will perhaps be compelled to bear such charges, but so far as other persons are concerned the right of fishing ought everywhere to be exempt from tolls, lest a servitude be imposed upon the sea, which is not susceptible to a servitude.

The case of the sea is not the same as that of a river,[2] for as a river is the property of a nation, the right to fish in it can be passed or leased by the nation or by the ruler, in such a way (and the like is true with the ancients) that the lessee enjoys the operation of the injunction *de loco publico fruendo* by virtue of the clause 'He who has the right to lease has leased the exclusive right of enjoyment'.[3] Such a condition cannot arise in respect to the sea. Finally those who count fishing among the properties of the Crown have not examined carefully enough the very passage which they cite to prove their contention, as Isernia * and Alvotus † have noticed.

It has therefore been demonstrated [4] that neither a nation nor an individual can establish any right of private owner-

[1] C. Quae sint Regalia, in Feudis.

[2] Balbus, De praescriptionibus IV, 5; 1, q. 6, n. 4.

[3] Digest XLVII, 10, 13; XLIII, 9, 1.

[4] See note 1.

* [Andrea d'Isernia (c. 1480-1553), an Italian commentator, called often Feudistarum Patriarcha.]

† [Probably a misprint for Alvarus (Alvarez).]

aliquod proprium in ipsum mare (nam diverticulum excipimus) competere posse, cum occupationem nec natura, nec usus publici ratio permittat. Huius autem rei causa instituta fuerat haec disputatio, ut appareret Lusitanos mare quo ad Indos navigatur sui iuris non fecisse. Nam utraque ratio quae proprietatem impedit, in hac causa est quam in ceteris omnibus infinito efficacior. Quod in aliis difficile videtur, in hac omnino fieri non potest; quod in aliis iniquum iudicamus, in hac summe barbarum est, atque inhumanum.

Non de mari interiore hic agimus, quod terris undique infusum alicubi etiam fluminis latitudinem non excedit, de quo tamen satis constat locutos Romanos Iurisconsultos, cum nobiles illas adversus privatam avaritiam sententias ediderunt; de Oceano quaeritur, quem immensum, infinitum, rerum parentem, caelo conterminum antiquitas vocat, cuius perpetuo humore non fontes tantum et flumina et maria, sed nubes, sed ipsa quodammodo sidera pasci veteres crediderunt; qui denique per reciprocas aestuum vices terram hanc humani generis sedem ambiens, neque teneri neque includi potest, et possidet verius quam possidetur.

In hoc autem Oceano non de sinu aut freto, nec de omni quidem eo quod e litore conspici potest controversia est. Vindicant sibi Lusitani quicquid duos Orbes interiacet, tantis spatiis discretos, ut plurimis saeculis famam sui non potuerint transmittere. Quod si Castellanorum, qui in eadem sunt

ship over the sea itself (I except inlets of the sea), inasmuch as its occupation is not permissible either by nature or on grounds of public utility. The discussion of this matter has been taken up for this reason, namely, that it may be seen that the Portuguese have not established private ownership over the sea by which people go to the East Indies. For the two reasons that stand in the way of ownership are in this case infinitely more powerful than in all others. That which in other cases seems difficult, is here absolutely impossible; and what in other cases we recognize as unjust is here most barbarous and inhuman.

The question at issue then is not one that concerns an INNER SEA, one which is surrounded on all sides by the land and at some places does not even exceed a river in breadth, although it is well known that the Roman jurists cited such an inner sea in their famous opinions condemning private avarice. No! the question at issue is the OUTER SEA, the OCEAN, that expanse of water which antiquity describes as the immense, the infinite, bounded only by the heavens, parent of all things; the ocean which the ancients believed was perpetually supplied with water not only by fountains, rivers, and seas, but by the clouds, and by the very stars of heaven themselves; the ocean which, although surrounding this earth, the home of the human race, with the ebb and flow of its tides, can be neither seized nor inclosed; nay, which rather possesses the earth than is by it possessed.

Further, the question at issue does not concern a gulf or a strait in this ocean, nor even all the expanse of sea which is visible from the shore. [But consider this!!] The Portuguese claim as their own the whole expanse of the sea which separates two parts of the world so far distant the one from the other, that in all the preceding centuries neither one has so much as heard of the other. Indeed, if we take into account the share of the Spaniards, whose claim

causa, portio accedat, parvo minus omnis Oceanus duobus populis mancipatus est, aliis tot gentibus ad Septentrionum redactis angustias; multumque decepta est Natura, quae cum elementum illud omnibus circumfudit, omnibus etiam suffecturum credidit. In tanto mari si quis usu promiscuo solum sibi imperium et dicionem exciperet, tamen immodicae dominationis affectator haberetur; si quis piscatu arceret alios, insanae cupiditatis notam non effugeret. At qui etiam navigatum impedit, quo nihil ipsi perit, de eo quid statuemus?

Si quis ab igni qui totus suus est, ignem capere, lumen suo de lumine, alterum prohiberet, lege hunc humanae societatis reum peragerem: quia vis ea est istius naturae:

Vt nihilominus ipsi luceat, cum illi accenderit.[1]

Quid ni enim quando sine detrimento suo potest, alteri communicet, in iis quae sunt accipienti utilia, danti non molesta.[2]

Haec sunt quae Philosophi[3] non alienis tantum, sed et ingratis praestari volunt. Quae vero in rebus privatis invidia est, eadem in re communi non potest non esse immanitas, improbissimum enim hoc est, quod naturae instituto, consensu gentium, meum non minus quam tuum est, id te ita intercipere, ut ne usum quidem mihi concedas, quo concesso nihilominus id tuum sit, quam antea fuit.

[1] Ennius: 'Nihilo minus ipsi lucet, cum illi accenderit'. Vahlen,[2] Fab. Inc. 398 (Telephus?).

[2] Cicero, De officiis I, 51.

[3] Seneca, De beneficiis III, 28 [IV, 28].

is the same as that of the Portuguese, only a little less than the whole ocean is found to be subject to two nations, while all the rest of the peoples in the world are restricted to the narrow bounds of the northern seas. Nature was greatly deceived if when she spread the sea around all peoples she believed that it would also be adequate for the use of them all. If in a thing so vast as the sea a man were to reserve to himself from general use nothing more than mere sovereignty, still he would be considered a seeker after unreasonable power. If a man were to enjoin other people from fishing, he would not escape the reproach of monstrous greed. But the man who even prevents navigation, a thing which means no loss to himself, what are we to say of him?

If any person should prevent any other person from taking fire from his fire or a light from his torch, I should accuse him of violating the law of human society, because that is the essence of its very nature, as Ennius has said:

"No less shines his, when he his friend's hath lit." [1]

Why then, when it can be done without any prejudice to his own interests, will not one person share with another things which are useful to the recipient, and no loss to the giver? [2] These are services which the ancient philosophers [3] thought ought to be rendered not only to foreigners but even to the ungrateful. But the same act which when private possessions are in question is jealousy can be nothing but cruelty when a common possession is in question. For it is most outrageous for you to appropriate a thing, which both by ordinance of nature and by common consent is as much mine as yours, so exclusively that you will not grant me a right of use in it which leaves it no less yours than it was before.

[1] [Quoted in Cicero, De officiis I, 51, and here taken from Walter Miller's (Loeb) translation, page 55.]

[2] Cicero, De officiis I, 51.

[3] Seneca, De beneficiis IV, 28.

Tum vero etiam qui alienis incumbunt, aut communia intercipiunt, certa quadam possessione se tuentur. Quia enim prima, ut diximus, occupatio res proprias fecit, idcirco imaginem quandam dominii praefert quamvis iniusta detentio. At Lusitani num sicuti terras solemus, sic mare illud impositis praediis ita undique cinxerunt, ut in ipsorum manu esset quos vellent excludere? An vero tantum hoc abest, ut ipsi etiam, cum adversus alios populos mundum dividunt, non ullis limitibus aut natura, aut manu positis, sed imaginaria quadam linea se tueantur? quod si recipitur et dimensio talis ad possidendum valet, iamdudum nobis Geometrae terras, Astronomi etiam caelum eriperent.

Vbi hic igitur est ista, sine qua nulla dominia coeperunt, corporis ad corpus adiunctio? Nimirum apparet in nulla re verius dici posse, quod Doctores nostri prodiderunt,[1] Mare cum sit incomprehensibile, non minus quam aër, nullius populi bonis potuisse applicari.

Si vero ante alios navigasse, et viam quodammodo aperuisse, hoc vocant occupare, quid esse potest magis ridiculum? Nam cum nulla pars sit maris, in quam non aliquis primus ingressus sit, sequetur omnem navigationem ab aliquo esse occupatam. Ita undique excludimur. Quin et illi qui terrarum orbem circumvecti sunt, totum sibi Oceanum acquisivisse dicendi erunt. Sed nemo nescit

[1] Johannes Faber on Institutes II, 1, 5 (De rerum divisione, § Litorum).

Nevertheless, even those who lay burdens upon foreigners, or appropriate things common to all, rely upon a possession which is to some extent real. For since original occupation created private property, therefore detention of a thing, though unjust, gives an appearance of ownership. But have the Portuguese completely covered the ocean, as we are wont to do on land, by laying out estates on it in such a way that they have the right to exclude from that ocean whom they will? Not at all! On the contrary, they are so far from having done so, that when they divide up the world to the disadvantage of other nations, they cannot even defend their action by showing any boundaries either natural or artificial, but are compelled to fall back upon some imaginary line. Indeed, if that were a recognized method, and such a delimitation of boundaries were sufficient to make possession valid, our geometers long since would have got possession of the face of the earth, our astronomers of the very skies.

But where in this case is that corporal possession or physical appropriation, without which no ownerships arise? There appears to be nothing truer than what our learned jurists have enunciated, namely,[1] that since the sea is just as insusceptible of physical appropriation as the air, it cannot be attached to the possessions of any nation.

But if the Portuguese call *occupying* the sea merely to have sailed over it before other people, and to have, as it were, opened the way, could anything in the world be more ridiculous? For, as there is no part of the sea on which some person has not already sailed, it will necessarily follow that every route of navigation is occupied by some one. Therefore we peoples of today are all absolutely excluded. Why will not those men who have circumnavigated the globe be justified in saying that they have acquired for themselves the possession of the whole ocean! But there

[1] Johannes Faber on Institutes II, 1, 5.

navem per mare transeuntem non plus iuris, quam vestigii relinquere. Verum etiam quod sibi sumunt neminem ante ipsos eum Oceanum navigasse, id minime verum est. Magna enim pars eius de quo agitur maris, ambitu Mauritaniae, iam olim navigata est; ulterior et in orientem vergens victoriis Magni Alexandri lustrata est, usque in Arabicum sinum.[1]

Olim autem hanc navigationem Gaditanis percognitam fuisse, multa argumento sunt. Caio Caesare Augusti filio in Arabico sinu res gerente signa navium ex Hispaniensibus naufragiis agnita. Et quod Caelius Antipater tradidit, vidisse se qui ex Hispania in Aethiopiam commercii gratia navigasset. Etiam Arabibus, si verum est, quod Cornelius Nepos testatus est, Eudoxum quendam sua aetate cum Lathyrum Regem Alexandriae fugeret, Arabico sinu egressum Gades usque pervectum. Poenos autem, qui re maritima plurimum valuerunt, eum Oceanum non ignorasse longe clarissimum est, cum Hanno Carthaginis potentia florente circumvectus a Gadibus ad finem Arabiae, praeternavigato scilicet promontorio quod nunc Bonae Spei dicitur, (vetus videtur nomen Hesperion ceras fuisse) omne id iter, situmque litoris et insularum scripto complexus sit, testatusque ad ultimum non mare sibi, sed commeatum defuisse.

Ab Arabico autem sinu ad Indiam, Indicique Oceani insulas, et auream usque Chersonesum, quam esse Iapanem credunt plerique, etiam re Romana florente navigari solitum, iter a Plinio descriptum,[2] legationes ab Indis ad

[1] Pliny, Naturalis historia II, 69; VI, 27 [(31) Vol. 1, pp. 482-488 Mayhoff]; Pomponius Mela, De situ orbis III.

[2] Pliny, Naturalis historia VI, 20 (23).

is not a single person in the world who does not know that a ship sailing through the sea leaves behind it no more legal right than it does a track. And as for the assumption of the Portuguese that no one has sailed that ocean before themselves, that is anything but true. For a great part of that sea near Morocco, which is in dispute, had already been navigated long before, and the sea as far east as the Arabian gulf has been made famous by the victories of Alexander the Great, as both Pliny and Mela tell us.[1]

There is also much to substantiate the belief that the inhabitants of Cadiz were well acquainted long ago with this route, because when Gaius Caesar,* the son of Augustus, held command in the Arabian gulf, pieces were found of shipwrecks recognized as Spanish. Caelius Antipater also has told us in his writings that he himself saw a Spaniard who had sailed from Spain to Ethiopia on a commercial voyage. Also the Arabians knew those seas, if the testimony of Cornelius Nepos is to be believed, because he says that in his own day a certain Eudoxus, fleeing from Lathyrus, king of Alexandria, sailed from the Arabian gulf and finally reached Cadiz. However, by far the most famous example is that of the Carthaginians. Those most famous mariners were well acquainted with that sea, because Hanno, when Carthage was at the height of her power, sailing from Cadiz to the farthest confines of Arabia, and doubling the promontory now known as the Cape of Good Hope (the ancient name seems to have been Hesperion Ceras), described in a book the entire route he had taken, the appearance of the coasts, and the location of the islands, declaring that at the farthest point he reached the sea had not yet given out but his provisions had.

Pliny's description of the route to the East,[2] the em-

[1] Pliny, Natural History II, 69; VI, 27; Pomponius Mela, De situ orbis III.

[2] Natural History VI, 20.

* [Strictly speaking, Gaius was the grandson of Augustus, but was adopted as his son.]

Augustum, ad Claudium etiam ex Taprobane insula, deinde gesta Traiani et tabulae Ptolemaei satis ostendunt. Iam suo tempore Strabo[1] Alexandrinorum mercatorum classem ex Arabico sinu, ut Aethiopiae ultima, ita et Indiae, petiisse testatur, cum olim paucis navibus id auderetur. Inde magna populo Romano vectigalia; addit Plinius[2] impositis sagittariorum cohortibus piratarum metu navigatum; solamque Indiam quingenties sestertium, si Arabiam addas et Seres, millies annis omnibus Romano Imperio ademisse; et merces centuplicato venditas.

Et haec quidem vetera satis arguunt primos non fuisse Lusitanos. In singulis autem sui partibus Oceanus ille et tunc cum eum Lusitani ingressi sunt, et numquam non cognitus fuit. Mauri enim, Aethiopes, Arabes, Persae, Indi, eam maris partem cuius ipsi accolae sunt, nescire neutiquam potuerunt.

Mentiuntur ergo qui se mare illud invenisse iactant.

Quid igitur, dicet aliquis, parumne videtur, quod Lusitani intermissam multis forte saeculis navigationem primi repararunt, et, quod negari non potest, Europaeis gentibus ignotam ostenderunt, magno suo labore, sumptu, periculo?

[1] Geographica II et XVII.
[2] Pliny, Naturalis historia XII, 19 [VI, 23].

bassies from the Indies to Augustus, and those from Ceylon to the emperor Claudius, and finally the accounts of the deeds of Trajan, and the writings of Ptolemaeus, all make it quite clear that in the days of Rome's greatest splendor voyages were made regularly from the Arabian gulf to India, to the islands of the Indian ocean, and even so far as to the golden Chersonesus, which many people think was Japan. Strabo says [1] that in his own time a fleet of Alexandrian merchantmen set sail from the Arabian gulf for the distant lands of Ethiopia and India, although few ships had ever before attempted that voyage. The Roman people had a large revenue from the East. Pliny says [2] that cohorts of archers were carried on the boats engaged in trade as protection against pirates; he states also that every year 500,000 sesterces * were taken out of the Roman empire by India alone, or 1,000,000 sesterces if you add Arabia and China; further, that merchandise brought from the East sold for one hundred times its original cost.

These examples cited from ancient times are sufficient proof that the Portuguese were not the first in that part of the world. Long before they ever came, every single part of that ocean had been long since explored. For how possibly could the Moors, the Ethiopians, the Arabians, the Persians, the peoples of India, have remained in ignorance of that part of the sea adjacent to their coasts!

Therefore they lie, who today boast that they discovered that sea.

Well then, some one will say, does it seem to be a matter of little moment that the Portuguese were the first to restore a navigation interrupted perhaps for many centuries, and unknown—as cannot be denied—at least to the nations of Europe, at great labor and cost and danger to them-

[1] Geography II and XVII.
[2] Natural History VI, 23.
* [A Roman sestertius was about four cents.]

Immo vero si in hoc incubuerunt ut quod soli reperissent id omnibus monstrarent, quis adeo est amens, qui non plurimum se illis debere profiteatur? Eandem enim gratiam, laudemque et gloriam immortalem illi promeruerint, qua omnes contenti fuerunt rerum magnarum inventores, quotquot scilicet non sibi, sed humano generi prodesse studuerunt. Sin Lusitanis suus ante oculos quaestus fuit, lucrum quod semper maximum est in praevertendis negotiationibus, illis sufficere debuit. Et scimus itinera prima proventus interdum quater decuplos, aut etiam uberiores dedisse, quibus factum ut inops diu populus ad repentinas divitias subito prorumperet, tanto luxus apparatu, quantus vix beatissimis gentibus in supremo progressae diu fortunae fastigio fuit.

Si vero eidem in hoc praeiverunt, ne quisquam sequeretur, gratiam non merentur, cum lucrum suum respexerint; lucrum autem suum dicere non possunt, cum eripiant alienum. Neque enim illud certum est nisi ivissent eo Lusitani, iturum fuisse neminem. Adventabant enim tempora, quibus ut artes paene omnes, ita et terrarum et marium situs clarius in dies noscebantur. Excitassent vetera, quae modo retulimus, exempla, et si non uno impetu omnia patuissent, at paulatim promota velis fuissent litora alio semper aliud monstrante. Factum denique fuisset,

selves? On the contrary, if they had laid weight upon the fact that they were pointing out to all what they alone had rediscovered, there is no one so lacking in sense that he would not acknowledge the greatest obligation to them. For the Portuguese will have earned the same thanks, praise, and immortal glory with which all discoverers of great things have been content, whenever they have striven to benefit not themselves but the whole human race. But if the Portuguese had before their eyes only their own financial gain, surely their profit, which is always the largest for those first in a new field of enterprise, ought to have satisfied them. For we know that their first voyages returned a profit sometimes of forty times the original investment, and sometimes even more. And by this overseas trade it has come about that a people, previously for a long time poor, have leaped suddenly into the possession of great riches, and have surrounded themselves with such outward signs of luxurious magnificence as scarcely the most prosperous nations have been able to display at the height of their fortunes.

But if these Portuguese have led the way in this matter in order that no one may follow them, then they do not deserve any thanks, inasmuch as they have considered only their own profit. Nor can they call it their profit, because they are taking the profit of some one else. For it is not at all demonstrable that, if the Portuguese had not gone to the East Indies, no one else would have gone. For the times were coming on apace in which along with other sciences the geographical locations of seas and lands were being better known every day. The reports of the expeditions of the ancients mentioned above had aroused people, and even if all foreign shores had not been laid open at a single stroke as it were, yet they would have been brought to light gradually by sailing voyages, each new discovery pointing the way to the next. And so there would finally

quod fieri potuisse Lusitani docuerunt, cum multi essent populi non minus flagrantes mercaturae et rerum externarum studio. Venetis qui multa iam Indiae didicerant, cetera inquirere promptum fuit. Gallorum Brittonum indefessa sedulitas, Anglorum audacia coepto non defuisset. Ipsi Batavi multo magis desperata aggressi sunt.

Nulla igitur aequitatis ratio, ne probabilis quidem ulla sententia a Lusitanis stat. Omnes enim qui mare volunt imperio alicuius subici posse, id ei attribuunt qui proximos portus et circumiacentia litora in dicione habet.[1] At Lusitani in illo immenso litorum tractu paucis exceptis praesidiis nihil habent quod suum possint dicere.

Deinde vero etiam qui Mari imperaret, nihil tamen posset ex usu communi deminuere, sicut Populus Romanus arcere neminem potuit, quo minus in litore imperi Romani cuncta faceret, quae iure gentium permittebantur.[2] Et si quicquam eorum prohibere posset, puta piscaturam qua dici quodammodo potest pisces exhauriri, at navigationem non posset, per quam mari nihil perit.

Cui rei argumentum est longe certissimum, quod ex Doctorum sententia ante retulimus, etiam in terra, quae cum populis, tum hominibus singulis in proprietatem attributa est, iter tamen, certe inerme et innoxium, nullius gentis

[1] Gloss. on Lib. VI, I, 6, 3 (De electione, c. Ubi periculum, § Porro); on Digest II, 12, 3 (De feriis, L. Solet [Grotius has Licet]).

[2] Digest I, 8, 4 (De divisione rerum, L. Nemo igitur); Gentilis, De jure belli I, 19.

have been accomplished what the Portuguese showed could be done, because there were many nations with no less ardor than theirs to engage in commerce and to learn of foreign things. The Venetians, who already knew much about India, were ready to push their knowledge farther; the indefatigable zeal of the French of Brittany, and the boldness of the English would not have failed to make such an attempt; indeed the Dutch themselves have embarked upon much more desperate enterprises.

Therefore the Portuguese have neither just reason nor respectable authority to support their position, for all those persons who assume that the sea can be subjected to the sovereignty of any one assign it to him who holds in his power the nearest ports and the circumjacent shores.[1] But in all that great extent of coast line reaching to the East Indies the Portuguese have nothing which they can call their own except a few fortified posts.

And then even if a man were to have dominion over the sea, still he could not take away anything from its common use, just as the Roman people could not prevent any one from doing on the shores of their dominions all those things which were permitted by the law of nations.[2] And if it were possible to prohibit any of those things, say for example, fishing, for in a way it can be maintained that fish are exhaustible, still it would not be possible to prohibit navigation, for the sea is not exhausted by that use.

The most conclusive argument on this question by far however is the one that we have already brought forward based on the opinions of eminent jurists, namely, that even over land which had been converted into private property either by states or individuals, unarmed and innocent passage is not justly to be denied to persons of any country, exactly as the right to drink from a river is not to be

[1] Glossators on Lib. VI, I, 6, 3; on Digest II, 12, 3.

[2] Digest I, 8, 4; Gentilis, De jure belli I, 19.

hominibus iuste negari; sicut et potum ex flumine. Ratio apparet, quia cum unius rei naturaliter usus essent diversi, eum dumtaxat gentes divisisse inter se videntur, qui sine proprietate commode haberi non potest, contra autem eum recepisse, per quem domini condicio deterior non esset futura.

Omnes igitur vident eum qui alterum navigare prohibeat nullo iure defendi, cum eundem etiam iniuriarum teneri Vlpianus dixerit;[1] alii autem etiam interdictum utile prohibito competere existimaverint.[2]

Et sic Batavorum intentio communi iure nititur, cum fateantur omnes, permissum cuilibet in mari navigare etiam a nullo Principe impetrata licentia; quod Legibus Hispanicis diserte expressum est.[3]

[1] Digest XLIII, 8, 2 (Ne quid in loco publico, L. Praetor ait, § Si quis in mari).

[2] Gloss. on Digest XLIII, 14 (Ut in flumine publico).

[3] Baldus on Digest I, 8, 3 (De divisione rerum, L. Item lapilli); Zuarius, Consilia duo de usu maris I, 3, part. tit. 28, L. 10 et 12.

denied. The reason is clear, because, inasmuch as one and the same thing is susceptible by nature to different uses, the nations seem on the one hand to have apportioned among themselves that use which cannot be maintained conveniently apart from private ownership; but on the other hand to have reserved that use through the exercise of which the condition of the owner would not be impaired.

It is clear therefore to every one that he who prevents another from navigating the sea has no support in law. Ulpian has said [1] that he was even bound to pay damages, and other jurists have thought that the injunction *utile prohibito* could also be brought against him.[2]

Finally, the relief prayed for by the Dutch rests upon a common right, since it is universally admitted that navigation on the sea is open to any one, even if permission is not obtained from any ruler. And this is specificially expressed in the Spanish laws.[3]

[1] Digest XLIII, 8, 2.

[2] Glossators on Digest XLIII, 14.

[3] Baldus on Digest I, 8, 3; Zuarius, Consilia duo de usu maris I, 3, 28, L. 10 and 12. [Rodericus Zuarius, Consilia published in 1621].

CAPVT VI

Mare aut ius navigandi proprium non esse Lusitanorum titulo donationis Pontificiae

Donatio Pontificis Alexandri, quae a Lusitanis mare aut ius navigandi solis sibi vindicantibus, cum inventionis deficiat titulus, secundo loco adduci potest, satis ex iis quae ante dicta sunt vanitatis convincitur. Donatio enim nullum habet momentum in rebus extra commercium positis. Quare cum mare aut ius in eo navigandi proprium nulli hominum esse possit, sequitur neque dari a Pontifice neque a Lusitanis accipi potuisse. Praeterea cum supra relatum sit ex omnium sani iudicii hominum sententia Papam non esse dominum temporalem totius orbis, ne Maris quidem esse satis intelligitur; quamquam etsi id concederetur, tamen ius annexum Pontificatui in Regem aliquem aut populum pro parte nulla transferri debuisset. Sicut nec Imperator posset Imperi provincias in suos usus convertere, aut pro suo arbitrio alienare.[1]

Illud saltem nemo negaturus est, cui aliquid sit frontis, cum ius disponendi in temporalibus Pontifici nemo concedat, nisi forte quantum eius rerum spiritualium necessitas requirit, ista autem de quibus nunc agimus, mare scilicet et ius navigandi, lucrum et quaestum merum, non pietatis negotium

[1] Victoria, De Indis I (II?), n. 26.

CHAPTER VI

Neither the Sea nor the right of navigation thereon belongs to the Portuguese by virtue of title based on the Papal Donation

The Donation of Pope Alexander, inasmuch as the title based on discovery is seen to be deficient, may next be invoked by the Portuguese to justify their exclusive appropriation of the sea and the right of navigation thereon. But from what has been said above, that Donation is clearly convicted of being an act of empty ostentation. For a Donation has no effect on things outside the realm of trade. Wherefore since neither the sea nor the right of navigating it can become the private property of any man, it follows that it could not have been given by the Pope, nor accepted by the Portuguese. Besides, as has been mentioned above, following the opinion of all men of sound judgment, it is sufficiently well recognized that the Pope is not the temporal lord of the earth, and certainly not of the sea. Even if it be granted for the sake of argument that such were the case, still a right attaching to the Pontificate ought not to be transferred wholly or in part to any king or nation. Similarly no emperor could convert to his own uses or alienate at his own pleasure the provinces of his empire.[1]

Now, inasmuch as no one concedes to the Pope in temporal matters a *jus disponendi,* except perhaps in so far as it is demanded by the necessity of spiritual matters, and inasmuch as the things now under discussion, namely, the sea and the right of navigating it, are concerned only with money and profits, not with piety, surely no one can have

[1] Victoria, De Indis I, n. 26.

respiciant, sequi nullam hac in re fuisse illius potestatem. Quid, quod ne Principes quidem, hoc est, domini temporales possunt ullo modo a navigatione aliquem prohibere, cum si quod habent ius in mari id sit tantum iurisdictionis ac protectionis? Etiam illud notissimum est apud omnes, ad ea facienda quae cum lege Naturae pugnant, nullam esse Papae auctoritatem.[1] Pugnat autem cum lege Naturae, ut mare aut eius usum quisquam habeat sibi proprium, ut iam satis demonstravimus. Cum denique ius suum auferre alicui Papa minime possit, quae erit facti istius defensio, si tot populos immerentes, indemnatos, innoxios ab eo iure quod ad ipsos non minus quam ad Hispanos pertinebat uno verbo voluit excludere?

Aut igitur dicendum est nullam esse vim eiusmodi pronuntiationis, aut quod non minus credibile est, eum Pontificis animum fuisse, ut Castellanorum et Lusitanorum inter se certamini intercessum voluerit, aliorum autem iuri nihil diminutum.

[1] Silvestris, In verbo Papa. n. 16.

the face to insist that the Pope had any jurisdiction here. What of the fact that not even rulers, that is to say, temporal lords, can prohibit any one from navigation, since if they have any right at all upon the sea it is merely one of jurisdiction and protection! It is also a fact universally recognized that the Pope has no authority to commit acts repugnant to the law of nature.[1] But it is repugnant to the law of nature, as we have already proved beyond a doubt, for any one to have as his own private property either the sea or its use. Finally, since the Pope is wholly unable to deprive any one of his own rights, what defense will there be for that Donation of his, if by a word he intended to exclude so many innocent, uncondemned, and guiltless nations from a right which belongs no less to them than to the Spaniards?

Therefore, either it must be affirmed that a pronunciamento of this sort has no force, or, as is no less credible, that it was the desire of the Pope to intercede in the quarrel between the Spaniards and the Portuguese, and that he had no concomitant intention of violating the rights of others.

[1] Silvestris, In verbo Papa. n. 16.

CAPVT VII

Mare aut ius navigandi proprium non esse Lusitanorum titulo praescriptionis aut consuetudinis

Vltimum iniquitatis patrocinium in praescriptione solet esse aut consuetudine. Et huc igitur Lusitani se conferunt; sed utrumque illis praesidium certissima iuris ratio praecludit. Nam praescriptio a iure est civili, unde locum habere non potest inter reges, aut inter populos liberos;[1] multo autem minus ubi ius naturae aut gentium resistit, quod iure civili semper validius est. Quin et ipsa lex civilis praescriptionem hic impedit.[2] Vsucapi enim, aut praescriptione acquiri prohibentur, quae in bonis esse non possunt, deinde quae possideri vel quasi possideri nequeunt, et quorum alienatio prohibita est. Haec autem omnia de mari et usu maris vere dicuntur.

Et cum publicae res, hoc est populi alicuius nulla temporis possessione quaeri posse dicantur, sive ob rei naturam, sive ob eorum privilegium adversus quos praescriptio ista procederet, quanto iustius humano generi, quam uni populo id beneficium dandum fuit in rebus communibus? Et hoc est

[1] Vasquius, Controversiae illustres, c. 51.

[2] Donellus, V, 22 et seq.; Digest XVIII, 1, 6 (De contrahenda emptione, L. Sed Celsus); XLI, 3, 9 (De usucapionibus, L. Usucapionem), 25 (L. Sine); Lib. VI, V, 12 (De regulis iuris, Reg. Sine possessione); Digest L, 16, 28 (De verborum significatione, L. 'Alienationis'); XXIII, 5, 16 (De fundo dotali, L. Si fundum).

CHAPTER VII

Neither the Sea nor the right of navigation thereon belongs to the Portuguese by title of prescription or custom

The last defense of injustice is usually a claim or plea based on prescription or on custom. To this defense therefore the Portuguese have resorted. But the best established reasoning of the law precludes them from enjoying the protection of either plea.

Prescription is a matter of municipal law; hence it cannot be applied as between kings, or as between free and independent nations.[1] It has even less standing when it is in conflict with that which is always stronger than the municipal law, namely, the law of nature or nations. Nay, even municipal law itself prevents prescription in this case.[2] For it is impossible to acquire by usucaption or prescription things which cannot become property, that is, which are not susceptible of possession or of quasi-possession, and which cannot be alienated. All of which is true with respect to the sea and its use.

And since public things, that is, things which are the property of a nation, cannot be acquired by mere efflux of time, either because of their nature, or because of the prerogatives of those against whom such prescription would act, is it not vastly more just that the benefits accruing from the enjoyment of common things should be given to the entire human race than to one nation alone? On this point

[1] Vasquius, Controversiae illustres, c. 51.

[2] Donellus, V. 22 ff.; Digest XVIII, 1, 6; XLI, 3, 9, 25; Lib. VI, V, 12 (Reg. Sine possessione); Digest L, 16, 28; XXIII, 5, 16.

quod Papinianus scriptum reliquit,[1] ' praescriptionem longae possessionis ad obtinenda loca iurisgentium publica concedi non solere '; eiusque rei exemplum dat in litore, cuius pars imposito aedificio occupata fuerat. Nam eo diruto, et alterius aedificio in eodem loco postea exstructo, exceptionem opponi non posse; quod deinde similitudine rei publicae illustrat, nam et si quis in fluminis diverticulo pluribus annis piscatus sit, postea, interrupta scilicet piscatione, alterum eodem iure prohibere non posse.

Apparet igitur Angelum et qui cum Angelo dixerunt[2] Venetis et Genuensibus per praescriptionem ius aliquod in sinum maris suo litori praeiacentem acquiri potuisse, aut falli, aut fallere, quod sane Iurisconsultis nimium est frequens, cum sanctae professionis auctoritatem, non ad rationes et leges, sed ad gratiam conferunt potentiorum. Nam Martiani quidem responsum, de quo et ante egimus, si recte cum Papiniani verbis comparetur,[3] non aliam accipere potest interpretationem, quam eam quae et Iohanni olim et Bartolo probata est, et nunc a doctis omnibus recipitur:[4] ut scilicet ius prohibendi procedat quamdiu durat occupatio,

[1] Digest XLI, 3, 45 (De usucapionibus); Code VIII, 11, 6 (De operis publicis, L. Praescriptio); XI, 43, 9 (De aquaeductu, L. Diligenter); Digest XLIII, 11, 2 (De via publica, L. Viam); XLI, 3, 49 (De usucapionibus, L. ult.).

[2] Consilia 286; Thema tale est: inter caetera capitula pacis.

[3] Digest XLIV, 3, 7 (De diversis temporalibus praescriptionibus, L. Si quisquam).

[4] Duarenus, De usucapionibus, c. 3; Cuiacius on Digest XLI, 3, 49 (De usucapionibus, L. ult.); Donellus V, 22 on Digest XLI, 1, 14 (De adquirendo rerum dominio, L. Quod in litore).

Papinian has said:[1] 'Prescription raised by long possession is not customarily recognized as valid in the acquisition of places known to international law as "public"'. As an example, to illustrate this point, he cites a shore some part of which had been occupied by means of a building constructed on it. But if this building should be destroyed, and some one else later should construct a building on the same spot, no exception could be taken to it. Then he illustrates the same point by the analogous case of a *res publica.* If, for example, any one has fished for many years in a branch of a river, and has then stopped fishing there, after that he cannot prevent any one else from enjoying the same right that he had.

Wherefore it appears that Angeli[2] and his followers who have said that the Venetians and Genoese were able to acquire by prescription certain specific rights in the gulfs of the sea adjacent to their shores, either are mistaken, or are deceiving others; a thing which happens all too frequently with jurists when they exercise the authority of their sacred profession not for justice and law, but in order to gain the gratitude of the powerful. There is also an opinion of Marcianus, already cited above in another connection, which, when carefully compared with the words of Papinian,[3] can have no other interpretation than the one formerly adopted by Johannes and Bartolus,* and now accepted by all learned men,[4] namely, that the *jus prohibendi* is in effect only while occupation lasts; it loses its force if occupation

[1] Digest XLI, 3, 45; Code VIII, 11, 6; XI, 43, 9; Digest XLIII, 11, 2; XLI, 3, 49.

[2] Consilia 286 [Angelus Aretinus a Gambellionibus (?-1445), a voluminous commentator on the Digest and the Institutes].

[3] Digest XLIV, 3, 7.

[4] Duren, De usucapionibus, c. 3; Cujas on Digest XLI, 3, 49; Donellus V, 22 on Digest XLI, 1, 14.

* [Bartolus de Saxoferrato (1314-1357) the most famous of the Post-glossators, was called by many of his biographers 'Optimus auriga in hac civili sapientia'.]

non autem si ea omissa sit; omissa enim non prodest, nec si per mille annos fuisset continuata, ut recte animadvertit Castrensis. Et quamvis hoc voluisset Martianus, quod minime credendus est cogitasse, in quo loco occupatio conceditur, in eodem praescriptionem concedi, tamen absurdum erat quod de flumine publico dictum erat ad Mare commune, et quod de diverticulo ad sinum proferre, cum haec praescriptio usum qui est Iuregentium communis, impeditura sit, illa autem publico usui non admodum noceat. Alterum autem Angeli argumentum quod ex aquaeductu sumitur,[1] eodem Castrensi monstrante, ut a quaestione alienissimum, ab omnibus merito exploditur.

Falsum igitur est talem praescriptionem etiam eo tempore gigni, cuius initium omnem memoriam excedat. Vbi enim lex omnem omnino tollit praescriptionem, ne istud quidem tempus admittitur, hoc est, ut Felinus loquitur,[2] materia impraescriptibilis tempore immemoriali non fit praescriptibilis. Fatetur haec vera esse Balbus;[3] sed Angeli sententiam receptam dicit hac ratione, quia tempus extra memoriam positum idem valere creditur privilegio, cum titulus amplissimus ex tali tempore praesumatur. Apparet hinc non aliud illos sensisse, quam si pars aliqua reipublicae, puta Imperi Romani, supra omnem memoriam usa esset tali iure, ei dandam praescriptionem hoc colore, quasi Principis

[1] Code XI, 43, 4 (De aquaeductu, L. Usum aquae); cf. eod. tit., L. Diligenter; cf. Digest XLIII, 20, 3 (De aqua cottidiana et aestiva, L. Hoc iure, § Ductus aquae).

[2] On Decretales Gregorii Papae IX, II, 26, 11 (De praescriptionibus, c. Accedentes).

[3] De praescriptionibus IV, 5, q. 6, n. 8.

cease; and occupation once interrupted, even if it had been continuous for a thousand years, loses its rights, as Paul de Castro * justly observes. And even if Marcianus had meant —which certainly was not in his mind at all—that acquisition by prescription is to be recognized wherever occupation is recognized, still it would have been absurd to apply what had been said about a public river to the common sea, or what had been said about an inlet or a river branch to a bay, since in the latter case prescription would hinder the use of something common to all by the law of nations, and in the former case would work no great injury to public use. Moreover, another argument brought forward by Angeli based on the use of aqueducts,[1] has quite properly been rejected by every one, being, as de Castro pointed out, entirely aside from the point.

It is not true then that such prescription rises even at a time beyond the period of the memory of man. For since the law absolutely denies all prescription, not even immemorial time has any effect on the question; that is, as Felinus [2] says, things imprescriptible by nature do not become prescriptible by the mere efflux of immemorial time. Balbus admits the truth of these arguments,[3] but says that the opinion of Angeli is to be accepted on the ground that time immemorial is believed to have the same validity as prerogative for setting up a title, since a perfect title is presumed from such efflux of time. Hence it appears that the jurists thought if some part of a state, say of the Roman empire for example, at a period before the memory of man had exercised such a right, that a title by prescription would

[1] Code XI, 43, 4; cf. XI, 43, 9; cf. Digest XLIII, 20, 3.

[2] On the Decretals of Pope Gregory IX, II, 26, 11 [Felinus Maria Sandeus (c. 1427-1503), Bishop of Lucca].

[3] De praescriptionibus IV, 5, q. 6, n. 8 [Johannes Franciscus Balbus, a priest and jurisconsult at Muentz-hof].

* [The celebrated Italian jurist (?-1420 or 1437) of whom Cujas said: "Si vous n'avez pas Paul de Castro, vendez votre chemise pour l'acheter." (Note from page 55 of the French translation of Grotius by de Grandpont.)]

concessio praeiisset. Quare cum nemo sit dominus totius generis humani, qui ius illud adversus homines omnes homini, aut populo alicui potuisset concedere, sublato illo colore, necesse est etiam praescriptionem interimi. Et sic ex illorum etiam sententia inter reges aut populos liberos prodesse nihil potest lapsus infiniti temporis.

Vanissimum autem et illud est quod Angelus docuit, etiamsi ad dominium praescriptio proficere non potest, tamen dandam esse possidenti exceptionem. Nam Papinianus disertis verbis exceptionem negat:[1] et aliter non potuit sentire, cum ipsius saeculo praescriptio nihil esset aliud quam exceptio. Verum igitur est quod et leges Hispanicae exprimunt[2] in his rebus quae communi hominum usui sunt attributae, nullius omnino temporis praescriptionem procedere, cuius definitionis illa praeter ceteras ratio reddi potest, quod qui re communi utitur, ut communi uti videtur, non autem iure proprio, et ita praescribere non magis quam fructuarius potest vitio possessionis.[3]

Altera haec etiam non contemnenda est, quod in praescriptione temporis cuius memoria non exstat, quamvis titulus et bona fides praesumantur, tamen si re ipsa appareat titulum omnino nullum dari posse, et sic manifesta sit fides mala, quae in populo maxime quasi uno corpore perpetua esse

[1] On Digest XLI, 3, 49 (De usucapionibus, L. ult.).

[2] Par. 3, tit. 29, l. 7 in c. Placa.; Zuarius, Consilia, num. 4.

[3] Fachinham VIII, c. 26 et c. 33; Duarenus, De praescriptionibus, parte 2, § 2, n. 8; § 8, n. 5 et 6.

have to be admitted on that ground, exactly as if there had been a previous grant from a Prince. But inasmuch as there is no one who is sovereign of the whole human race with competence to grant to any man or to any nation such a right against all other men, with the annihilation of that pretext, title by prescription is also necessarily destroyed. Therefore the opinion of the jurists is that not even an infinite lapse of time is able to set up a right as between kings or independent nations.

Moreover Angeli brought forward a most foolish argument, affirming that even if prescription could not create ownership, still an exception ought to be made in favor of a possessor. Papinian however in unmistakable words says there is no exception,[1] nor could he think otherwise, because in his day prescription was itself an exception. It is therefore true, as expressed also in the laws of Spain,[2] that prescription based on no matter how immemorial a time, sets up no title to those things which are recognized as common to the use of mankind. One reason among others which can be given for this definition is that any one who uses a *res communis* does so evidently by virtue of common and not private right, and because of the imperfect character of possession he can therefore no more set up a legal title by prescription than can a usufructuary.[3]

A second reason not to be overlooked is that although a title and good faith are presumed in a prescriptive right created by the efflux of immemorial time, nevertheless if it appears from the nature of the thing itself that no title at all can be established, and if thus there becomes evident bad faith—a thing held to be permanent in a nation as well as in an individual—then prescription fails because of a

[1] On Digest XLI, 3, 49.

[2] Par. 3, tit. 29, 1. 7 in c. Placa.; Zuarius, Consilia, num. 4.

[3] Fachinham VIII, c. 26 and c. 33; Duaren, De praescriptionibus, parte 2, § 2, n. 8; § 8, n. 5 and 6. [Nicholas Fachinham (?-1407), a Franciscan, who taught Theology at Oxford.]

censetur, et ex duplici defectu praescriptio corruit.[1] Tertia vero, quia res haec est merae facultatis, quae non praescribitur, ut infra demonstrabimus.

Sed nullus est finis argutiarum. Inventi sunt qui in hoc argumento a praescriptione consuetudinem distinguerent, ut illa scilicet exclusi, ad hanc confugerent. Discrimen autem quod hic statuunt sane ridiculum est: ex praescriptione aiunt ius unius quod ab eo aufertur alteri applicari;[2] sed cum aliquod ius ita alicui applicatur ut alteri non auferatur, tum dici consuetudinem; quasi vero cum ius navigandi quod communiter ad omnes pertinet, exclusis aliis ab uno usurpatur, non necesse sit omnibus perire quantum uni accedit. Errori huic ansam dederunt Pauli verba non recte accepta, qui cum de iure proprio maris ad aliquem pertinente loqueretur,[3] fieri hoc posse dixit Accursius per privilegium aut consuetudinem: quod additamentum ad Iurisconsulti textum nullo modo accedens mali potius coniectoris esse videtur quam boni interpretis. Mens Pauli supra explicata est. Ceterum illi si vel sola Vlpiani verba,[4] quae paulo ante praecedunt, satis considerassent, longe aliud dicturi erant. Fatetur enim ut quis ante aedes meas piscari prohibeatur, esse quidem usur-

[1] Fachinham VIII, c. 28.

[2] Angelus Aretinus in rubr. Digest I, 8 (De divisione rerum); Balbus, l. c., n. 2; cf. Vasquium, Controversiae illustres c. 29, n. 38.

[3] On Digest XLVII, 10, 14 (De iniuriis, L. Sane).

[4] Digest XLVII, 10, 13 (De iniuriis, L. Iniuriarum, § ult.)

double defect.[1] Also a third reason is that we have under consideration a merely facultative right which is not prescriptible, as we shall show below.*

But there is no end to their subtilties. There are jurists who in this case would distinguish custom from prescription, so that if they are debarred from the one, they may fall back upon the other. But the distinction which they set up is most absurd. They say that the right of one person which is taken away from him is given to another by prescription;[2] but that when any right is given to any one in such a way that it is not taken away from any one else, then it is called custom. As if indeed the right of navigation, which is common to all, upon being usurped by some one to the exclusion of all others, would not necessarily when it became the property of one be lost to all!

This error receives support from misinterpretation of what Paulus has to say about a private right of possession on the sea.[3] Accursius † said that such a right could be acquired by privilege or custom. But this addition which in no way agrees with the text of the jurist seems to be rather the interpretation of a mischievous guesser than of a faithful interpreter. The real meaning of the words of Paulus has been already explained. Besides, if more careful consideration had been given to the words of Ulpian[4] which almost immediately precede those of Paulus, a very different assertion would have been made. For Ulpian acknowledges that if any one is prohibited from fishing in front of

[1] Fachinham VIII, c. 28.

[2] Angelus Aretinus on Digest I, 8; Balbus, De praescriptionibus IV, 5, q. 6, n. 2; see Vasquius, Controversiae illustres c. 29, n. 38.

[3] On Digest XLVII, 10, 14.

[4] Digest XLVII, 10, 13.

* [See chapter XI.]

† [Franciscus (?) Accursius (?-1259) (a pupil of the famous Monarcha juris Azzo), with whose name the Glossa Magna is almost synonymous. He was called Advocatorum Idolum.]

patum;[1] hoc est receptum consuetudine, sed nullo iure, ideoque iniuriarum actionem prohibito non denegandam.

Contemnit igitur hunc morem, et usurpationem vocat, ut et inter Christianos Doctores Ambrosius.[2] Et merito. Quid enim clarius quam non valere consuetudinem, quae iuri naturae, aut gentium ex adverso opponitur?[3] Consuetudo enim species est iuris positivi, quod legi perpetuae obrogare non potest. Est autem lex illa perpetua ut Mare omnibus usu commune sit. Quod autem in praescriptione diximus, idem in consuetudine verum est, si quis eorum qui diversum tradiderunt sensus excutiat, non aliud reperturum, quam consuetudinem privilegio parari. Atqui adversus genus humanum concedendi privilegium nemo habet potestatem; quare inter diversas respublicas consuetudo ista vim non habet.

Verum omnem hanc quaestionem diligentissime tractavit Vasquius,[4] decus illud Hispaniae, cuius nec in explorando iure subtilitatem, nec in docendo libertatem umquam desideres. Is igitur posita thesi: ‘ Loca publica et iure gentium communia praescribi non posse ’, quam multis firmat auctoribus; exceptiones deinde subiungit ab Angelo et aliis confictas, quas supra retulimus. Haec autem examinaturus recte iudicat istarum rerum veritatem pendere a vera iuris, tam naturae quam gentium cognitione. Ius enim naturae cum a

[1] Cf. Gloss. eodem loco.
[2] De officiis ministrorum I, 28; Gentilis I, 19 (sub finem).
[3] Auth. Ut nulli Iudicum § 1, c. cum tanto de consuetudine.
[4] Controversiae illustres c. 89, n. 12 et seq.

my house, such prohibition is a usurpation of right,[1] allowed, it is true, by custom, but based on no law, and that an action for damages could not be denied the person thus prohibited from fishing.

He therefore condemns this practice, and calls it a usurpation; of the Christian jurists Ambrose[2] does likewise, and both are right. For what is clearer than that custom is not valid when it is diametrically opposed to the law of nature or of nations?[3] Indeed, custom is a sort of affirmative right, which cannot invalidate general or universal law. And it is a universal law that the sea and its use is common to all. Moreover what we have said about prescription applies with equal truth and force to custom; and if any one should investigate the opinions of those who have differed upon this matter, he would find no other opinion but that custom is established by privilege. No one has the power to confer a privilege which is prejudicial to the rights of the human race; wherefore such a custom has no force as between different states.

This entire question however has been most thoroughly treated by Vasquez,[4] that glory of Spain, who leaves nothing ever to be desired when it comes to subtle examination of the law or to the exposition of the principles of liberty. He lays down this thesis: 'Places public and common to all by the law of nations cannot become objects of prescription'. This thesis he supports by many authorities, and then he subjoins the objections fabricated by Angeli and others, which we have enumerated above. But before examining these objections he makes the just and reasonable statement that the truth of all these matters depends upon a true conception both of the law of nature and the law of nations.

[1] Glossators on the reference in note 4, page 51.

[2] De officiis ministrorum I, 28; Gentilis I, 19.

[3] Auth. Ut nulli Iudicum § 1, c. cum tanto de consuetudine.

[4] Controversiae illustres c. 89, n. 12 ff. [Ferdinand Manchaea Vasquez (1509-1566) the famous Spanish jurisconsult, who held many high honors of the realm].

divina veniat providentia, esse immutabile. Huius autem iuris naturalis partem esse ius gentium, primaevum quod dicitur, diversum a iure gentium secundario sive positivo, quorum posterius mutari potest. Nam si qui mores cum iure gentium primaevo repugnent, hi non humani sunt ipso iudice, sed FERINI, corruptelae et abusus, non leges et usus. Itaque nullo tempore praescribi potuerunt, nulla lata lege iustificari, nullo multarum etiam gentium consensu, hospitio, et exercitatione stabiliri, quod exemplis aliquot et Alphonsi Castrensis Theologi Hispani testimonio confirmat.[1]

'Ex quibus apparet', inquit, 'quam suspecta sit sententia eorum, quos supra retulimus, existimantium Genuenses, aut etiam Venetos posse non iniuria prohibere alios navigare per Gulfum aut pelagus sui maris, quasi aequora ipsa praescripserint, id quod non solum est contra leges,[2] sed etiam est contra ipsum ius naturae, aut gentium primaevum, quod mutari non posse diximus. Quod sit contra illud ius constat, quia non solum maria aut aequora eo iure communia erant sed etiam reliquae omnes res immobiles. Et licet ab eo iure postea recessum fuerit ex parte, puta quoad dominium et proprietatem terrarum, quarum dominium iure Naturae commune, distinctum et divisum, sicque ab illa communione segregatum fuit; tamen [3] diversum fuit et est in dominio maris,

[1] De potestate legis poenalis II, 14, part. 572.

[2] Digest XLI, 1, 14 (De adquirendo rerum dominio, L. Quod in litore); XLI, 3 (De usucapionibus, L. fin. in prin.); Institutes II, 1, 2 (De rerum divisione, § Flumina, v. omnibus); Digest XLIV, 3, 7 (De diversis temporalibus praescriptionibus, L. Si quisquam); XLVII, 10, 14 (De iniuriis, L. Sane si maris).

[3] Digest I, 1, 5 (De iustitia et iure, L. Ex hoc iure); Institutes I, 2 (De iure naturali et gentium et civili, § 2, v. ius autem gentium).

For, since the law of nature arises out of Divine Providence, it is immutable; but a part of this natural law is the primary or primitive law of nations, differing from the secondary or positive law of nations, which is mutable. For if there are customs incompatible with the primary law of nations, then, according to the judgment of Vasquez, they are not customs belonging to men, but to wild beasts, customs which are corruptions and abuses, not laws and usages. Therefore those customs cannot become prescriptions by mere lapse of time, cannot be justified by the passage of any law, cannot be established by the consent, the protection, or the practice even of many nations. These statements he confirms by a number of examples, and particularly by the testimony of Alphonse de Castro [1] the Spanish theologian.

'It is evident therefore', he says, 'how much to be suspected is the opinion of those persons mentioned above, who think that the Genoese or the Venetians can without injustice prohibit other nations from navigating the gulfs or bays of their respective seas, as if they had a prescriptive right to the very water itself. Such an act is not only contrary to the laws,[2] but is contrary also to natural law or the primary law of nations, which we have said is immutable. And this is seen to be true because by that same law not only the seas or waters, but also all other immovables were *res communes*. And although in later times there was a partial abandonment of that law, in so far as concerns sovereignty and ownership of lands—which by natural law at first were held in common, then distinguished and divided, and thus finally separated from the primitive community of use;—nevertheless [3] it was different as regards sovereignty over the sea, which from the beginning of the world down to this

[1]De potestate legis poenalis II, 14, part 572 [Alphonse de Castro (?-1558). Theologian at Salamanca, confessor to the Emperor Charles V.].

[2] Digest XLI, 1, 14; XLI, 3; Institutes II, 1, 2; Digest XLIV, 3, 7; XLVII, 10, 14.

[3] Digest I, 1, 5; Institutes I, 2, § 2.

quod ab origine Mundi, ad hodiernum usque diem est, fuitque semper in communi, nulla ex parte immutatum, ut est notum'.

'Et quamvis ex LVSITANIS magnam turbam saepe audiverim in hac esse opinione ut eorum Rex ita praescripserit navigationem INDICI Occidentalis (forte Orientalis) eiusdemque VASTISSIMI MARIS, ita ut reliquis gentibus aequora illa transfretare non liceat, et ex nostrismet HISPANIS VVLGVS in eadem opinione fere esse videtur, ut per VASTISSIMVM IMMENSVMQVE PONTVM ad Indorum regiones quas potentissimi Reges nostri subegerunt reliquis mortalium navigare praeterquam Hispanis ius minime sit, quasi ab eis id ius praescriptum fuerit, tamen istorum omnium non minus INSANAE sunt opiniones, quam eorum qui quoad Genuenses et Venetos in eodem fere SOMNIO esse adsolent, quas sententias INEPTIRE vel ex eo dilucidius apparet, quod istarum nationum singulae contra seipsas nequeunt praescribere: hoc est, non respublica Venetiarum contra semetipsam, non respublica Genuensium contra semetipsam, non Regnum Hispanicum contra semetipsum, non Regnum Lusitanicum contra semetipsum.[1] Esse enim debet differentia inter agentem et patientem'.

'Contra reliquas vero nationes longe minus praescribere possunt, quia ius praescriptionum est mere civile, ut fuse ostendimus supra. Ergo tale ius cessat cum agitur inter principes vel populos, superiorem non recognoscentes in temporalibus. Iura enim mere civilia cuiuscumque regionis,

[1] Digest XLI, 3, 4, 26 (27) (De usucapionibus, L. Sequitur § Si viam); Institutes IV, 6, 14 (De actionibus, § Sic itaque); Ut dictis iuribus et L. cum filio, ubi multa per Bartolum et Jason on Digest XXX, 11 (De Legatis I, L. Cum filio; part. I in pr. qu. 3 et 4).

very day is and always has been a *res communis,* and which, as is well known, has in no wise changed from that status.

'And although', he continues, 'I have often heard that a great many Portuguese believe that their king has a prescriptive right over the navigation of the vast seas of the West Indies (probably the East Indies too) such that other nations are not allowed to traverse those waters; and although the common people among our own Spaniards seem to be of the same opinion, namely, that absolutely no one in the world except us Spaniards ourselves has the least right to navigate the great and immense sea which stretches to the regions of the Indies once subdued by our most powerful kings, as if that right has been ours alone by prescription; although, I repeat, I have heard both these things, nevertheless the belief of all those people is no less extravagantly foolish than that of those who are always cherishing the same delusions with respect to the Genoese and Venetians. Indeed the opinions of them all appear the more manifestly absurd, because no one of those nations can erect a prescription against itself; that is to say, not the Venetian republic, nor the Genoese republic, nor the kingdom of Spain nor of Portugal can raise prescriptions against rights they already possess by nature.[1] For the one who claims a prescriptive right and the one who suffers by the establishment of such a claim must not be one and the same person.

'Against other nations they are even much less competent to raise a prescription, because the right of prescription is only a municipal right, as we have shown above at some length. Therefore such a right ceases to have any effect as between rulers or nations who do not recognize a superior in the temporal domain. For so far as the merely municipal laws of any place are concerned, they do not

[1] Digest XLI, 3, 4, 26 (27); Institutes IV, 6, 14; Bartolus and Jason on Digest XXX, 11.

quoad exteros populos, nationes, vel etiam homines singulos, non magis sunt in consideratione, quam si re vera esset tale ius, aut numquam fuisset, et ad ius commune gentium primaevum vel secundarium recurrendum est, eoque utendum, quo iure talem maris praescriptionem et usurpationem admissam non fuisse satis constat. Nam, et hodie usus aquarum communis est, non secus quam erat ab origine Mundi. Ergo et in aequoribus et aquis nullum ius est aut esse potest humano generi, praeterquam quoad usum communem. Praeterea de iure naturali et divino est illud praeceptum, ut *Quod tibi non vis fieri, alteri non facias.* Vnde cum navigatio nemini possit esse nociva nisi ipsi naviganti, par est ut nemini possit, aut debeat impediri, ne in re sua natura libera, sibique minime noxia navigantium libertatem impediat, et laedat contra dictum praeceptum et contra regulam praesertim cum omnia intelligantur esse permissa, quae non reperiuntur expressim prohibita.[1] Quinimo non solum contra ius naturale esset, velle impedire talem navigationem, sed etiam tenemur contrarium facere, hoc est, prodesse iis quibus possumus, cum id sine damno nostro fieri potest'.

Quod cum multis auctoritatibus tam divinis quam humanis confirmasset, subiungit postea:[2] 'Ex superioribus etiam apparet suspectam esse sententiam Iohannis Fabri, Angeli, Baldi, et Francisci Balbi, quos supra retulimus, existimantium loca iuris gentium communia, et si acquiri non possint praescriptione, posse tamen acquiri consuetudine,

[1] Digest I, 5, 4 (De statu hominum, L. Libertas); Institutes I, 3, 1 (De iure personarum, § Et libertas); Digest XLIII, 29, 1 et 2 (De homine libero exhibendo); XLIV, 5, 1 (Quarum rerum actio non datur, L. Iusiurandum, § Quae onerandae); Code III, 28, 35 (De inofficioso testamento, L. Si quando, § Illud, v. adstringendos); Digest IV, 6, 28 (Ex quibus causis maiores, L. Nec non, § 'Quod eius').

[2] Code III, 44, 7 (De religiosis et sumptibus funerum, L. Statuas).

affect foreign peoples, nations, or even individuals, any more than if they did not exist or never had existed. Therefore it was necessary to have recourse to the common law of nations, primary as well as secondary, and to use a law which clearly had not admitted any such prescription and usurpation of the sea. For today the use of the waters is common, exactly as it has been since the creation of the world. Therefore no man has a right nor can acquire a right over the seas and waters which would be prejudicial to their common use. Besides, there is both in natural and divine law that famous rule: 'Whatsoever ye would that men should not do to you, do not ye even so to them'. Hence it follows, since navigation cannot harm any one except the navigator himself, it is only just that no one either can or ought to be interdicted therefrom, lest nature, free in her own realm, and least hurtful to herself, be found impeding the liberty of navigation, and thus offending against the accepted precept and rule that all things are supposed to be permitted which are not found expressly forbidden.[1] Besides, not only would it be contrary to natural law to wish to prevent such free navigation, but we are even bound to do the opposite, that is, bound to assist such navigation in whatever way we can, when it can be done without any prejudice to ourselves'.

After Vasquez had established his point by the help of many authorities both human and divine, he added:[2] 'It appears then, from what has gone before that the opinion held by Johannes Faber, Angeli, Baldus, and Franciscus Balbus, whom we have cited above, is not to be trusted, because they think that places common by the law of nations, even if not open to acquisition by prescription, can nevertheless be acquired by custom; but this is entirely false, and

[1] Digest I, 5, 4; Institutes I, 3, 1; Digest XLIII, 29, 1-2; XLIV, 5, 1; Code III, 28, 35; Digest IV, 6, 28.

[2] Code III, 44, 7.

quod omnino FALSVM est, eaque traditio CAECA ET NVBILA est, OMNIQVE RATIONIS LVMINE CARENS, legemque verbis non rebus imponens.[1] In exemplis enim de Mari Hispanorum, LVSITANORVM, Venetorum, Genuensium, et reliquorum, constat consuetudine ius tale navigandi, et alios navigare prohibendi non magis acquiri quam praescriptione.[2] Vtroque enim casu ut apparet, eadem est ratio. Et quia per iura et rationes supra relatas id esset contra naturalem aequitatem, nec ullam induceret utilitatem, sed solam laesionem, sicque ut lege expressa introduci non possent, ita etiam nec lege tacita, qualis est consuetudo.[3] Et tempore id non iustificaretur, sed potius deterius et iniurius in dies fieret'.

Ostendit deinde ex prima terrarum occupatione posse populo ut venandi ius, ita piscandi in suo flumine competere, et postquam illa semel ab antiqua communione separata sunt, ita ut particularem applicationem admittant, praescriptione temporis eius, cuius initi memoria non exstet, quasi tacita populi concessione acquiri posse. Hoc autem per praescriptionem contingere, non per consuetudinem, quia solius acquirentis condicio melior fiat, reliquorum vero deterior. Et cum tria enumerasset quae requiruntur, ut ius proprium in flumine piscandi praescribatur:

'Quid autem', subdit, 'quoad mare? Et in eo magis est

[1] Code VI, 43 (Communia de legatis, Contra L. 2, cum vulgatis).

[2] Digest IX, 2, 32 (Ad legem Aquiliam, L. Illud).

[3] Dist. IV, C II (Erit autem lex); Digest I, 3, 1 et 2 (De legibus), 32 (eod. tit., L. De quibus, cum seq.); Decretales Gregorii Papae IX, II, 26, 20 (De praescriptionibus, c. Quoniam).

is a teaching which is both obscure and vague, which lacks the faintest glimmer of reasonableness, and which sets up a law in word but not in fact.[1] For it is well established from the examples taken from the seas of the Spaniards, Portuguese, Venetians, Genoese, and others, that an exclusive right of navigation and a right of prohibiting others from navigation is no more to be acquired by custom than by prescription.[2] And it is apparent that the reason is the same in both cases. And since according to the laws and reasons adduced above this would be contrary to natural equity and would not bring benefit but only injury, therefore as it could not be introduced by an express law, neither could it be introduced by a tacit or implied law, and that is what custom is.[3] And far from justifying itself by any lapse of time, it rather becomes worse, and every day more injurious'.

Vasquez next shows that from the time of the earliest occupation of the earth every people possessed the right of hunting in its own territory, and of fishing in its own rivers. After those rights were once separated from the ancient community of rights in such a way that they admitted of particular attachments, they could be acquired by prescription based upon such an efflux of time that "the memory of its beginning does not exist," as if by the tacit permission of a nation. This comes about, however, by prescription and not by custom, because only the condition of him who acquires is bettered, while that of all other persons is made worse. Then after Vasquez had enumerated three conditions which are requisite in order that a private right of fishing in a river may become a right by prescription, he continues as follows:

'But what are we to say as regards the sea? There is

[1] Code VI, 43.
[2] Digest IX, 2, 32.
[3] Dist. IV, C. II; Digest I, 3, 1-2, 32; Decretals of Pope Gregory IX, II, 26, 20.

quod etiam concursus istorum trium non sufficeret ad acquirendum ius. Ratio differentiae inter mare ex una parte, et terram et flumina ex altera, quia illo casu ut olim ita et hodie, et semper, tam quoad piscandum quam quoad navigandum mansit integrum ius gentium primaevum, neque umquam fuit a communione hominum separatum, et alicui, vel aliquibus applicatum. Posteriore autem casu, nempe in terra vel fluminibus aliud fuit, ut iam disseruimus '.

'Sed quare ius gentium secundarium, ut eam separationem quoad terras et flumina facit, quoad mare facere desiit? respondeo, quia illo casu expediebat. Constat enim quod si multi venentur, aut piscentur in terra vel flumine, facile nemus feris, et flumen piscibus evacuatum redditur, id quod in mari non est. Item fluminum navigatio facile deterior fit et impeditur per aedificia, quod in mari non est. Item per aquaeductus facile evacuatur flumen, non ita in mari; [1] ergo in utroque non est par ratio '.

'Nec ad rem pertinet, quod supra diximus, communem esse usum aquarum, fontium etiam et fluminum. Nam intelligitur quoad bibendum et similia, quae fluminis dominium aut ius habenti vel minime vel levissime nocent.[2] Minima enim in consideratione non sunt. Pro nostris sententiis facit, quia iniqua nullo tempore praescribuntur, et ideo lex iniqua nullo tempore praescribitur, aut iustificatur '. Mox: 'Et

[1] Digest XLIII, 13 (Ne quid in flumine publico fiat).
[2] Digest IV, 4, 3 (De minoribus, L. 3, § Scio); Vasquius, De successionum progressu I, 7.

more to say about it, because even the combination of the three conditions mentioned is not sufficient here for the acquisition of such a right. The reason for the difference between the sea on one hand and land and rivers on the other, is that in the case of the sea the same primitive right of nations regarding fishing and navigation which existed in the earliest times, still today exists undiminished and always will, and because that right was never separated from the community right of all mankind, and attached to any person or group of persons. But in the latter case, that of the land and rivers, it was different, as we have already set forth.

'But why, it is asked, does the secondary law of nations which brings about this separation when we consider lands and rivers cease to operate in the same way when we consider the sea? I reply, because in the former case it was expedient and necessary. For every one admits that if a great many persons hunt on the land or fish in a river, the forest is easily exhausted of wild animals and the river of fish, but such a contingency is impossible in the case of the sea. Again, the navigation of rivers is easily lessened and impeded by constructions placed therein, but this is not true of the sea. Again, a river is easily emptied by means of aqueducts but the sea cannot be emptied by any such means.[1] Therefore there is not equal reason on both sides.

'Neither does what we have said above about the common use of waters, springs, and rivers, apply in this case, for common use is recognized in them all for purposes of drinking and the like, such usages namely as do not injure at all or in the slightest degree him who owns a river or has some other right in one.[2] These are trifles for which we have no time. What makes for our contention is the fact that no lapse of time will give a prescriptive right to anything unjust. Therefore an unjust law is not capable of

[1] Digest XLIII, 13.
[2] Digest IV, 4, 3; Vasquius, De successionum progressu I, 7.

quae sunt impraescriptibilia ex legis dispositione, nec per mille annos praescriberentur'; quod innumeris doctorum testimoniis fulcit.[1]

Nemo iam non videt, ad usum rei communis intercipiendum nullam quantivis temporis usurpationem prodesse. Cui adiungendum est etiam eorum qui dissentiunt auctoritatem huic quaestioni non posse accommodari. Illi enim de Mediterraneo loquuntur, nos de Oceano; illi de sinu, nos de immenso mari, quae in ratione occupationis plurimum differunt. Et quibus illi indulgent praescriptionem, illi litora mari continua possident, ut Veneti et Genuenses, quod de Lusitanis dici non posse modo patuit.

Immo et si prodesse posset tempus, ut quidam posse putant in publicis quae sunt, populi, tamen non ea adsunt quae necessario requiruntur. Primum enim docent omnes desiderari, ut is qui praescribit huiusmodi actum, eum exercuerit non longo dumtaxat tempore, sed memoriam excedente; deinde ut tanto tempore eundem actum nemo alius exercuerit, nisi concessione illius, vel clandestine; praeterea ut alios uti volentes prohibuerit, scientibus quidem et patien-

[1] Balbus, De praescriptionibus 5 in pr. in qu. 11, illius 5, quaest. pr. Gl. in cap. inter caetera 16, q. 3; Castrensis, De potestate legis poenalis II, 14; Balbus, and Angelus, on Code VII, 39, 4 (De praescriptione XXX vel XL annorum, L. Omnes).

erecting a prescriptive right or of being justified by efflux of time'. A little farther on Vasquez says: 'Things which are imprescriptible by the disposition of the law, may not become objects of prescription even after the lapse of a thousand years'. This statement he supports by countless citations from the jurists.[1]

Every one perceives that no usurpation no matter how long continued is competent to intercept the use of a *res communis.* And it must also be added, that the authority of those who hold dissenting opinions cannot possibly be applied to the question here at issue. For they are talking about the Mediterranean, we are talking about the Ocean; they speak of a gulf, we of the boundless sea; and from the point of view of occupation these are wholly different things. And too, those peoples, to whom the authorities just mentioned concede prescription, the Venetians and Genoese for example, possess a continuous shore line on the sea, but it is clear that not even that kind of possession can be claimed for the Portuguese.

Further, even if mere lapse of time, as some think, could establish a right by prescription over public property, still the conditions absolutely indispensable for the creation of such a right are in this case absent. The conditions demanded are these: first, all jurists teach that he who sets up a prescriptive right of this sort shall have been in actual possession not only for a considerable period, but from time immemorial; next, that during all that time no one else shall have exercised the same right of possession unless by permission of that possessor or clandestinely; besides that, it is necessary that he shall have prevented other persons wishing to use his possession from so doing, and that such measures be a matter of common knowledge and done by the suffrance of those concerned in the matter. For even if

[1] Balbus, De praescriptionibus 5, 11; 16, 3; Alphonse de Castro, De potestate legis poenalis II, 14; Balbus and Angelus on Code VII, 39, 4.

tibus iis ad quos ea res pertinebat; nam etsi exercuisset semper, et quosdam exercere volentes prohibuisset semper, non tamen omnes, quia alii fuerunt prohibiti, alii vero libere exercuerunt, id quidem ňon sufficeret, ex Doctorum sententia.

Apparet autem debere haec omnia concurrere, tum quia praescriptioni publicarum rerum lex inimica est, tum ut videatur praescribens iure suo non autem communi usus, idque non interrupta possessione.

Cum autem tempus postulatur, cuius initi non exstet memoria, non semper sufficit, ut optimi interpretes ostendunt, probare saeculi lapsum; sed constare oportet famam rei a maioribus ad nos transmissam, ita ut nemo supersit qui contrarium viderit, aut audierit. Occasione rerum Africanarum in ulteriora primum Oceani inquirere coeperunt regnante Iohanne Lusitani,[1] anno salutis millesimo quadringentesimo septuagesimo septimo. Viginti post annis, sub Rege Emanuele promontorium Bonae spei praeternavigatum est, seriusque multo ventum Malaccam, et insulas remotiores, ad quas Batavi navigare coeperunt anno millesimo quingentesimo nonagesimo quinto, non dubie intra annum centesimum. Iam vero etiam eo quod intercessit tempore aliorum usurpatio adversus alios etiam omnes impedivit praescriptionem. Castellani ab anno millesimo quingentesimo decimo nono possessionem Lusitanis maris circa Moluccas ambiguam

[1] Osorius, De rebus Emmanuelis regis Lusitaniae I.

he had continuously exercised his right of possession, and had always prevented from using his possession *some* of those who wished to do so, but not *all;* then, because *some* had been prevented from exercising and *others* freely allowed to exercise that use, that kind of possession according to the opinion of the jurists, is not sufficient to establish a right by prescription.

It is clear therefore that all these conditions should be present, both because law is opposed to the prescription of public things, and in order that he who sets up such a prescription may seem to have used his own private right, not a public right, and that too by continuous possession.

Now, inasmuch as time beyond the period of the memory of man is demanded for the creation of a prescriptive right, it is not always sufficient, as the best commentators point out, to prove the lapse of a hundred years, but the tradition handed down to us by our ancestors ought to be undisputed, provided no one is left alive who has seen or heard anything to the contrary. It was during the reign of King John,[1] in the year of our Lord 1477, at the time of the wars in Africa, that the Portuguese began to push their discoveries first into the more distant parts of the Ocean. Twenty years later, during the reign of King Emmanuel, they rounded the Cape of Good Hope, and somewhat later yet, reached Malacca, and the islands beyond, the very islands, indeed, to which the Dutch began to sail in the year 1595, that is, well within a hundred years of the time that the Portuguese first arrived. And in truth even in that interval, the usurpation of rights there by other parties had interrupted the competence of everybody else to create a prescriptive right. For example, from the year 1519, the Spaniards rendered the possession by the Portuguese of the sea around the Moluccas a very uncertain one. Even the French and

[1] Osorius, De rebus Emmanuelis regis Lusitaniae I [Hieronymus Osorius (1506-1580) was known as the Portuguese Cicero].

fecere. Galli etiam et Angli non clanculum, sed via aperta eo perruperunt. Praeterea accolae totius tractus Africani, aut Asiatici partem maris quisque sibi proximam piscando et navigando perpetuo usurparunt, numquam a Lusitanis prohibiti.

Conclusum igitur sit, ius nullum esse Lusitanis quo aliam quamvis gentem a navigatione Oceani ad Indos prohibeant.

English made their way to those newly discovered places not secretly, but by force of arms. And besides these, the inhabitants of the entire coast of Africa and Asia constantly used for fishing and navigation that part of the sea nearest their own several coasts, and were never interdicted from such use by the Portuguese.

The conclusion of the whole matter therefore is that the Portuguese are in possession of no right whereby they may interdict to any nation whatsoever the navigation of the Ocean to the East Indies.

CAPVT VIII

Iure gentium inter quosvis liberam esse mercaturam

Quod si dicant Lusitani cum Indis commercia exercendi ius quoddam proprium ad se pertinere, eisdem fere omnibus argumentis refellentur. Repetemus breviter et aptabimus.

Iure Gentium hoc introductum est, ut cunctis hominibus inter se libera esset negotiandi facultas, quae a nemine posset adimi.[1] Et hoc, sicut post dominiorum distinctionem continuo necessarium fuit, ita originem videri potest antiquiorem habuisse. Subtiliter enim Aristoteles *μεταβλητικὴν* dixit, *ἀναπλήρωσιν τῆς κατὰ φύσιν αὐταρκείας*,[2] hoc est, negotiatione suppleri id quod naturae deest, quo commode omnibus sufficiat. Oportet igitur communem esse iure gentium non tantum privative, sed et positive, ut dicunt magistri, sive affirmative.[3] Quae autem illo modo sunt iuris gentium, mutari possunt: quae hoc modo, non possunt. Id ita intelligi potest.

Dederat natura omnia omnibus. Sed cum a rerum multarum usu, quas vita desiderat humana, locorum intervallo homines arcerentur, quia ut supra diximus, non omnia ubique

[1] Digest I, 1, 5 (De iustitia et iure, L. Ex hoc iure); et ibi Bartolus.

[2] Aristotle, Politica I, 9 (1257a 30).

[3] Cf. Covarruvias in c. Peccatum, § 8.

CHAPTER VIII

By the Law of Nations trade is free to all persons whatsoever

If however the Portuguese claim that they have an exclusive right to trade with the East Indies, their claim will be refuted by practically all the same arguments which already have been brought forward. Nevertheless I shall repeat them briefly, and apply them to this particular claim.

By the law of nations the principle was introduced that the opportunity to engage in trade, of which no one can be deprived,[1] should be free to all men. This principle, inasmuch as its application was straightway necessary after the distinctions of private ownerships were made, can therefore be seen to have had a very remote origin. Aristotle, in a very clever phrase, in his work entitled the Politics,[2] has said that the art of exchange is a completion of the independence which Nature requires. Therefore trade ought to be common to all according to the law of nations, not only in a negative but also in a positive, or as the jurists say, affirmative sense.[3] The things that come under the former category are subject to change, those of the latter category are not. This statement is to be explained in the following way.

Nature had given all things to all men. But since men were prevented from using many things which were desirable in every day life because they lived so far apart,

[1] Digest I, 1, 5.
[2] I, 9 (1257a 30).
[3] Cf. Co~arruvias in c. Peccatum, § 8.

proveniunt, opus fuit traiectione; nec adhuc tamen permutatio erat, sed aliis vicissim rebus apud alios repertis suo arbitrio utebantur; quo fere modo apud Seres dicitur rebus in solitudine relictis sola mutantium religione peragi commercium.[1]

Sed cum statim res mobiles monstrante necessitate, quae modo explicata est, in ius proprium transisssent, inventa est permutatio, qua quod alteri deest ex eo quod alteri superest suppleretur.[2] Ita commercia victus gratia inventa ex Homero Plinius probat.[3] Postquam vero res etiam immobiles in dominos distingui coeperunt, sublata undique communio non inter homines locorum spatiis discretos tantum, verum etiam inter vicinos necessarium fecit commercium; quod ut facilius procederet, nummus postea adinventus est, dictus *ἀπὸ τοῦ νόμου* quod institutum sit civile.[4]

Ipsa igitur ratio omnium contractuum universalis, *ἡ μεταβλητική* a natura est; modi autem aliquot singulares ipsumque pretium, *ἡ χρηματιστική* ab instituto;[5] quae vetustiores iuris interpretes non satis distinxerunt. Fatentur

[1] Pomponius Mela, De situ orbis III, 7.

[2] Digest XVIII, 1, 1 (De contrahenda emptione, L. Origo).

[3] Naturalis historia XXXIII, 1.

[4] Aristotle, Ethica Nicomachea 5, 5, 11 (1133a 20): *οὐ φύσει ἀλλὰ νόμῳ ἐστί*; Politica I, 9 (1257b 10).

[5] Dist. I, C. VII (Ius naturale); Aristotle, l. c.

and because, as we have said above, everything was not found everywhere, it was necessary to transport things from one place to another; not that there was yet an interchange of commodities, but that people were accustomed to make reciprocal use of things found in one another's territory according to their own judgment. They say that trade arose among the Chinese in about this way. Things were deposited at places out in the desert and left to the good faith and conscience of those who exchanged things of their own for what they took.[1]

But when movables passed into private ownership (a change brought about by necessity, as has been explained above), straightway there arose a method of exchange by which the lack of one person was supplemented by that of which another person had an over supply.[2] Hence commerce was born out of necessity for the commodities of life, as Pliny shows by a citation from Homer.[3] But after immovables also began to be recognized as private property, the consequent annihilation of universal community of use made commerce a necessity not only between men whose habitations were far apart but even between men who were neighbors; and in order that trade might be carried on more easily, somewhat later they invented money, which, as the derivation of the word shows, is a civic institution.[4]

Therefore the universal basis of all contracts, namely exchange, is derived from nature; but some particular kinds of exchange, and the money payment itself, are derived from law;[5] although the older commentators on the law have not made this distinction sufficiently clear. Nevertheless all

[1] Pomponius Mela, De situ orbis III, 7.

[2] Digest XVIII, 1, 1.

[3] Natural History XXXIII, 1.

[4] Aristotle, Nicomachean Ethics 5, 5, 11 (1133a 20); Politics I, 9 (1257b 10) [Nummus = νόμος. The fact that this is an incorrect derivation does not of course affect the argument].

[5] Dist. I, C. VII; Aristotle, see note 4 above.

tamen omnes proprietatem rerum, saltem mobilium a iure gentium primario prodire, itemque contractus omnes quibus pretium non accedit.[1] Philosophi[2] *τῆς μεταβλητικῆς* quam translationem vertere licebit, genera statuunt duo: *τὴν ἐμπορικὴν καὶ τὴν καπηλικήν* quarum *ἐμπορική* quae ut vox ipsa indicat inter gentes dissitas, ordine naturae prior est, et sic a Platone ponitur.[3] *Καπηλική* eadem videtur esse quae *παράστασις*[4] Aristoteli, tabernaria sive stataria negotiatio inter cives. Idem Aristoteles[5] *τὴν ἐμπορικὴν* dividit in *ναυκληρίαν* et *φορτηγίαν* quarum haec terrestri itinere, illa maritimo merces devehit. Sordidior autem est *καπηλική* contra honestior *ἐμπορική* et maritima maxime, quia multa multis impertit.[6]

Vnde navium exercitionem ad summam rempublicam pertinere dicit Vlpianus; institorum non eundem esse usum; quia illa omnino secundum naturam necessaria est. Aristoteles:[7] *ἔστι γὰρ ἡ μεταβλητικὴ πάντων, ἀρξαμένη τὸ μὲν πρῶτον ἐκ τοῦ κατὰ φύσιν, τῷ τὰ μὲν πλείω, τὰ δὲ ἐλάττω τῶν ἱκανῶν ἔχειν τοὺς ἀνθρώπους,* ' est enim translatio rerum omnium coepta ab initio, ab eo quod est secundum naturam, cum homines partim haberent plura, quam sufficerent, partim etiam pauciora '. Seneca:[8] ' quae emeris, vendere; gentium ius est '.

Commercandi igitur libertas ex iure est primario gen-

[1] Castrensis ex Cino et aliis n. 20 et 28 on Digest I, 1, 5 (De iustitia et iure, L. Ex hoc iure).

[2] Plato, Sophista 223d.

[3] Plato, Republic II (p. 371) cited in Digest L, 11, 2 (De nundinis).

[4] Politica I, 11 (1258b 22-23).

[5] *καὶ ταύτης μέρη τρία, ναυκληρία, φορτηγία, παράστασις* are the exact words.

[6] Cicero, De officiis I, 150-151; Aristotle, Politica I, 9.

[7] L. c. (1257a 14-17).

[8] De beneficiis V, 8.

authorities agree that the ownership of things, particularly of movables, arises out of the primary law of nations, and that all contracts in which a price is not mentioned, are derived from the same source.[1] The philosophers [2] distinguish two kinds of exchange using Greek words which we shall take the liberty to translate as 'wholesale' and 'retail' trade. The former, as the Greek word shows, signifies trade or exchange between widely separated nations, and it ranks first in the order of Nature, as is shown in Plato's Republic.[3] The latter seems to be the same kind of exchange that Aristotle calls by another Greek word [4] which means retail or shop trade between citizens. Aristotle makes a further division of wholesale trade into overland and overseas trade.[5] But of the two, retail trade is the more petty and sordid, and wholesale the more honorable; but most honorable of all is the wholesale overseas trade, because it makes so many people sharers in so many things.[6]

Hence Ulpian says that the maintenance of ships is the highest duty of a state, because it is an absolutely natural necessity, but that the maintenance of hucksters has not the same value. In another place Aristotle says: "For the art of exchange extends to all possessions, and it arises at first in a natural manner from the circumstance that some have too little, others too much." [7] And Seneca is also to be cited in this connection for he has said that buying and selling is the law of nations.[8]

Therefore freedom of trade is based on a primitive right of nations which has a natural and permanent cause; and

[1] Castrensis from Cinus and others on Digest I, 1, 5.

[2] Plato, Sophista 223d.

[3] II (p. 371) cited in Digest L, 11, 2.

[4] Politics I, 11 (1258b 22-23).

[5] [The text here is somewhat expanded.]

[6] Cicero, De officiis I, 150-151; Aristotle, Politics I, 9.

[7] Politics I, 9 (1257a 14-17) [Jowett's translation, Vol. I, page 15].

[8] De beneficiis V, 8 [Not a quotation, but a summing up of the chapter].

tium, quod naturalem et perpetuam causam habet, ideoque tolli non potest, et si posset non tamen posset nisi omnium gentium consensu: tantum abest ut ullo modo gens aliqua gentes duas inter se contrahere volentes iuste impediat.

so that right cannot be destroyed, or at all events it may not be destroyed except by the consent of all nations. For surely no one nation may justly oppose in any way two nations that desire to enter into a contract with each other.

CAPVT IX

Mercaturam cum Indis propriam non esse Lusitanorum titulo occupationis

Primum inventio aut occupatio hic locum non habet, quia ius mercandi non est aliquid corporale, quod possit apprehendi; neque prodesset Lusitanis etiamsi primi hominum cum Indis habuissent commercia, quod tamen non potest non esse falsissimum. Nam et cum initio populi in diversa iere, aliquos necesse est primos fuisse mercatores, quos tamen ius nullum acquisivisse certo est certius. Quare si Lusitanis ius aliquod competit, ut soli cum Indis negotientur, id exemplo ceterarum servitutum, ex concessione oriri debuit aut expressa aut tacita, hoc est praescriptione; neque aliter potest.

CHAPTER IX

Trade with the East Indies does not belong to the Portuguese by title of occupation

Neither discovery nor occupation [which have been fully treated in Chapters II and V], is to be invoked on the point here under consideration, because the right of carrying on trade is not something corporal, which can be physically seized; nor would discovery or occupation help the case of the Portuguese even if they had been the very first persons to trade with the East Indies, although such a claim would be entirely untenable and false. For since in the beginning peoples set out along different paths, it was necessary that some become the first traders, nevertheless it is absolutely certain that those traders did not on that account acquire any rights. Wherefore if the Portuguese have any right by virtue of which they *alone* may trade with the East Indies, that right like other servitudes ought to arise from concession, either express or tacit, that is to say, from prescription. Otherwise no such right can exist.

CAPVT X

Mercaturam cum Indis propriam non esse Lusitanorum titulo donationis Pontificiae

Concessit nemo, nisi forte Pontifex, qui non potuit.[1] Nemo enim quod suum non est concedere potest. At Pontifex, nisi totius Mundi temporalis sit Dominus, quod negant sapientes, ius etiam commerciorum universale sui iuris dicere non potest. Maxime vero cum res sit ad solum quaestum accommodata, nihilque ad spiritualem procurationem pertinens, extra quam cessat, ut fatentur omnes, Pontificia potestas. Praeterea si Pontifex solis illud Lusitanis ius tribuere vellet idemque adimere hominibus ceteris, duplicem faceret iniuriam: Primum Indis, quos ut extra Ecclesiam positos Pontifici nulla ex parte subditos esse diximus. His igitur cum nihil quod ipsorum est adimere possit Pontifex, etiam ius illud quod habent cum quibuslibet negotiandi adimere non potuit. Deinde aliis hominibus omnibus Christianis et non Christianis, quibus idem illud ius adimere non potuit sine causa indicta. Quid quod ne temporales quidem Domini in suis imperiis prohibere possunt commerciorum libertatem, uti rationibus et auctoritatibus ante demonstratum est?

Sicut et illud confitendum est, contra ius perpetuum naturae gentiumque, unde ista libertas originem sumpsit in omne tempus duratura, nullam valere Pontificis auctoritatem.

[1] Cf. cap. III et VI.

CHAPTER X

Trade with the East Indies does not belong to the Portuguese by virtue of title based on the Papal Donation

No one has granted it except perhaps the Pope, and he did not have the power.[1] For no one can give away what he does not himself possess. But the Pope, unless he were the temporal master of the whole world, which sensible men deny, cannot say that the universal right in respect of trade belongs to him. Especially is this true since trade has to do only with material gains, and has no concern at all with spiritual matters, outside of which, as all admit, Papal power ceases. Besides, if the Pope wished to give that right to the Portuguese alone, and to deprive all other men of the same right, he would be doing a double injustice. In the first place, he would do an injustice to the people of the East Indies who, placed as we have said outside the Church, are in no way subjects of the Pope. Therefore, since the Pope cannot take away from them anything that is theirs, he could not take away their right of trading with whomsoever they please. In the second place, he would do an injustice to all other men both Christian and non-Christian, from whom he could not take that same right without a hearing. Besides, what are we to say of the fact that not even temporal lords in their own dominions are competent to prohibit the freedom of trade, as has been demonstrated above by reasonable and authoritative statements?

Therefore it must be acknowledged, that the authority of the Pope has absolutely no force against the eternal law of nature and of nations, from whence came that liberty which is destined to endure for ever and ever.

[1] See chapters III and VI.

CAPVT XI

Mercaturam cum Indis non esse Lusitanorum propriam iure praescriptionis aut consuetudinis

Restat praescriptio, seu consuetudinem mavis dicere.[1] Sed nec huius nec illius vim esse aliquam inter liberas nationes, aut diversarum gentium Principes, nec adversus ea quae primigenio iure introducta sunt, cum Vasquio ostendimus. Quare et hic ut ius mercandi proprium fiat, quod proprietatis naturam non recipit, nullo tempore efficitur. Itaque nec titulus hic adfuisse potest, nec bona fides, quae cum manifesto desinit, praescriptio secundum Canones non ius dicetur, sed iniuria.

Quin et ipsa mercandi quasi possessio non ex iure proprio contigisse videtur, sed ex iure communi quod ad omnes aequaliter pertinet; sicut contra, quod aliae nationes cum Indis contrahere forte neglexerunt, id non Lusitanorum gratia fecisse existimandi sunt, sed quia sibi expedire crediderunt; quod nihil obstat quo minus ubi suaserit utilitas, id facere possint, quod antea non fecerint. Certissima enim illa regula a doctoribus traditur,[2] in his quae sunt arbitrii seu merae facultatis, ita ut per se actum tantum facultatis eius, non autem ius novum operentur, nec praescriptionis nec consuetudinis titulo annos etiam mille valituros: quod et

[1] Cf. cap. VII.

[2] Gloss. et Bartolus on Digest XLIII, 11, 2 (De via publica, L. Viam publicam); Balbus 4, 5 pr. qu. 1; Panormitanus on Decretales Gregorii Papae IX, III, 8, 10 (De concessione praebendae, c. Ex parte Hastenen.); Digest XLI, 2, 41 (De adquirenda possessione, L. Qui iure familiaritatis); Covarruvias in c. possessor. 2, § 4; Vasquius, Controversiae illustres c. 4, n. 10 et 12.

CHAPTER XI

Trade with the East Indies does not belong to the Portuguese by title of prescription or custom

Last of all, prescription, or if you prefer the term, custom.[1] We have shown that according to Vasquez, neither prescription nor custom had any force as between free nations or the rulers of different peoples, or any force against those principles which were introduced by primitive law. And here as before, mere efflux of time does not bring it to pass that the right of trade, which does not partake of the nature of ownership, becomes a private possession. Now in this case neither title nor good faith can be shown, and inasmuch as good faith is clearly absent, according to legal rules prescription will not be called a right, but an injury.

Nay, the very possession involved in trading seems not to have arisen out of a private right, but out of a public right which belongs equally to all; so on the other hand, because nations perhaps neglected to trade with the East Indies, it must not be presumed that they did so as a favor to the Portuguese, but because they believed it to be to their own best interests. But nothing stands in their way, when once expediency shall have persuaded them, to prevent them from doing what they had not previously done. For the jurists [2] have handed down as incontestable the principle that where things arbitrable or facultative are such that they produce nothing more than the facultative act *per se,* but do not create a new right, that in all such cases not even a thousand years will create a title by prescription or custom.

[1] See chapter VII.

[2] On Digest XLIII, 11, 2; Balbus 4, 5 pr. qu. 1; Panormitanus on the Decretals of Pope Gregory IX, III, 8, 10; Digest XLI, 2, 41; Covarruvias in c. possessor. 2, § 4; Vasquius, Controversiae illustres c. 4, n. 10 and 12.

affirmative et negative procedit, ut docet Vasquius. Nec enim quod libere feci facere cogor, nec quod non feci omittere.

Alioquin quid esset absurdius quam ex eo quod singuli non possumus cum singulis semper contrahere, salvum nobis in posterum non esse ius cum illis, si usus tulerit, contrahendi? Idem Vasquius et illud rectissime, ne infinito quidem tempore effici, ut quid necessitate potius, quam sponte factum videatur.

Probanda itaque Lusitanis foret coactio, quae tamen ipsa cum hac in re iuri naturae sit contraria, et omni hominum generi noxia, ius facere non potest.[1] Deinde illa coactio durasse debuit per tempus, cuius initii non exstet memoria; id vero tantum hinc abest, ut ne centum quidem anni exierint, ex quo tota fere negotiatio Indica penes Venetos fuit, per Alexandrinas traiectiones.[2] Debuit etiam talis esse coactio, cui restitum non sit. At restiterunt Galli et Angli, aliique. Neque sufficit aliquos esse coactos, sed ut omnes coacti sint requiritur, cum per unum non coactum servetur in causa communi libertatis possessio. Arabes autem et Sinenses a saeculis aliquot ad hunc usque diem perpetuo cum Indis negotiantur.

Nihil prodest ista usurpatio.

[1] Vasquius, l. c. n. 11.
[2] Guicciardini, Storia d'Italia XIX.

This, as Vasquez points out, acts both affirmatively and negatively. For I am not compelled to do what I have hitherto done of my own free will, nor am I compelled to stop doing what I have never done.

What moreover could be more absurd then to deduce from the fact that we as individuals are not able always to conclude a bargain with other individuals, that there is not preserved to us for the future the right of bargaining with them if opportunity shall have offered? The same Vasquez has also most justly said that not even the lapse of infinite time establishes a right which seems to have arisen from necessity rather than choice.

Therefore in order to establish a prescriptive right to the trade with the East Indies the Portuguese would be compelled to prove coercion. But since in such a case as this coercion is contrary to the law of nature and obnoxious to all mankind, it cannot establish a right.[1] Next, that coercion must needs have been in existence for so long a time that "the memory of its beginning does not exist"; that, however, is so far from being the case that not even a hundred years had elapsed since the Venetians controlled nearly the entire trade with the East Indies, carrying it via Alexandria.[2] Again, the coercion ought to have been such that it was not resisted; but the English and the French and other nations besides, did resist it. Finally, it is not sufficient that *some* be coerced, but it is indispensable that *all* be coerced, because the possession of freedom of trade is preserved to all by a failure to use coercion upon even one person. Moreover, the Arabians and the Chinese are at the present day still carrying on with the people of the East Indies a trade which has been uninterrupted for several centuries.

Portuguese usurpation is worthless.

[1] Vasquius, Controversiae illustres c. 4, n. 11.
[2] Guicciardini, Storia d'Italia XIX.

CAPVT XII

Nulla aequitate niti Lusitanos in prohibendo commercio

Ex his quae dicta sunt satis perspicitur eorum caeca aviditas, qui, ne quemquam in partem lucri admittant, illis rationibus conscientiam suam placare student, quas ipsi magistri Hispanorum qui in eadem sunt causa manifestae vanitatis convincunt.[1] Omnes enim qui in rebus Indicis usurpantur colores iniuste captari quantum ipsis licet, satis innuunt, adduntque numquam eam rem serio Theologorum examine probatam. Illa vero querela quid est iniquius, quod dicunt Lusitani quaestus suos exhauriri copia contra licentium? Inter certissima enim Iuris enuntiata est, nec in dolo eum versari, nec fraudem facere, ne damnum quidem alteri dare videri, qui iure suo utitur; quod maxime verum est, si non ut alteri noceatur, sed rem suam augendi animo quippiam fiat.[2] Inspici enim debet id quod principaliter agitur, non quod extrinsecus in consequentiam venit. Immo si proprie loquimur cum Vlpiano, non ille damnum dat, sed lucro quo adhuc alter utebatur eum prohibet.

Naturale autem est et summo iuri atque etiam aequitati

[1] Vasquius, Controversiae illustres c. 10, n. 10; Victoria, De Indis I, 1, n. 3; Digest VI, 1, 27 (De rei vindicatione, L. Sin autem, § penult.) L, 17, 55 et 151 (De diversis regulis, L. Nullus videtur, et L. Nemo damnum); XLII, 8, 13 (Quae in fraudem creditorum, L. Illud constat); XXXIX, 2, 24 (De damno infecto, L. Fluminum, § ult.); Bartolus on Digest XLIII, 12, 1 (De fluminibus, L. 1, § 5); Castrensis on Code III, 34, 10 (De servitutibus, L. Si tibi); Digest XXXIX, 3, 1 (De aqua, L. Si cui, § Denique).

[2] Vasquius, Controversiae illustres c. 4, n. 3 et seq.; Digest XXXIX, 2, 26 (De damno infecto, L. Proculus).

CHAPTER XII

The Portuguese prohibition of trade has no foundation in equity

From what has been said thus far it is easy to see the blind cupidity of those who in order not to admit any one else to a share in their gains, strive to still their consciences by the very arguments which the Spanish jurists, interested too in the same case, show to be absolutely empty.[1] For they intimate as clearly as they can that as regards India all the pretexts employed, are far fetched and unjust. They add that this right was never seriously approved by the swarm of theologians. Indeed, what is more unjust than the complaint made by the Portuguese that their profits are drained off by the number of their competitors? An incontrovertible rule of law lays down that a man who uses his own right is justly presumed to be contriving neither a deceit nor a fraud, in fact not even to be doing any one an injury. This is particularly true, if he has no intention to harm any one, but only to increase his own property.[2] For what ought to be considered is the chief and ultimate intent not the irrelevant consequence. Indeed, if we may with propriety agree with Ulpian, he is not doing an injury, but he is preventing some one from getting a profit which another was previously enjoying.

Moreover it is natural and conformable to the highest law as well as equity, that when a gain open to all is concerned every person prefers it for himself rather than for

[1] Vasquius, Controversiae illustres c. 10, n. 10; Victoria, De Indis I, 1, n. 3; Digest VI, 1. 27; L, 17, 55, 151; XLII, 8, 13; XXXIX, 2, 24; Bartolus on Digest XLIII, 12, 1; Castrensis on Code III, 34, 10; Digest XXXIX, 3, 1.

[2] Vasquius, Controversiae illustres c. 4, n. 3 ff.; Digest XXXIX, 2, 26.

conveniens, ut lucrum in medio positum suum quisque malit quam alterius, etiam qui ante perceperat.[1] Quis ferat querentem opificem quod alter eiusdem artis exercitio ipsius commoda evertat? Batavorum autem causa eo est iustior, quia ipsorum hac in parte utilitas cum totius humani generis utilitate coniuncta est, quam Lusitani eversum eunt.[2] Neque hoc recte dicetur ad aemulationem fieri, ut in re simili ostendit Vasquius: aut enim plane hoc negandum est, aut asseverandum non ad bonam modo, verum etiam ad optimam aemulationem fieri, iuxta Hesiodum:[3] *ἀγαθὴ δ' Ἔρις ἥδε βροτοῖσι* ' bona lis mortalibus haec est '. Nam etiam si quis pietate motus, inquit ille, frumentum in summa penuria vilius venderet, impediretur improba duritie eorum hominum, qui saeviente penuria suum carius fuerant vendituri. Verum est talibus modis minui aliorum reditus: nec id negamus, ait, ' sed minuuntur cum universorum hominum commodo: ET VTINAM omnium PRINCIPVM et TYRRANORVM ORBIS reditus ita minuerentur '.

Quid ergo tam iniquum videri potest, quam Hispanos vectigalem habere Terrarum Orbem, ut nisi ad illorum nutum nec emere liceat nec vendere?[4] In cunctis civitatibus dardanarios odio atque etiam poenis prosequimur; nec ullum tam nefarium vitae genus videtur, quam ista annonae flagellatio.[5] Merito quidem. Naturae enim faciunt

[1] Vasquius, l. c.
[2] Vasquius, l. c. n. 5.
[3] Ἐργα καὶ Ἡμέραι 24.
[4] Code IV, 59 (De monopoliis, L. 1).
[5] Caietanus on Thomas Aquinas, Summa II. II, q. 77, a. 1, ad 3.

another, even if that other had already discovered it.[1] Who would countenance an artisan who complained that another artisan was taking away his profits by the exercise of the same craft? But the cause of the Dutch is the more reasonable, because their advantage in this matter is bound up with the advantage of the whole human race, an advantage which the Portuguese are trying to destroy.[2] Nor will it be correct to say, that this is done in rivalry, as Vasquez shows in a similar case. For clearly we must either deny this or affirm that it is done not only in honorable but in most honorable rivalry, for, as Hesiod says, 'This rivalry is honorable for mortal men'.[3] For, says Vasquez, if any one should be so moved by love for his fellow man as to offer grain at a time of great scarcity for a lower price than usual, he would be prevented by the wicked and hardhearted men who had the intention of selling their grain at a higher price than usual, because of the pinch caused by the scarcity. But, some one will object, by such methods the profits of others will be made less. 'We do not deny it', says Vasquez, 'but they are made less to the corresponding advantage of all other men. And would that the profits of all Rulers and Tyrants of this world could be thus lessened'!

Indeed can anything more unjust be conceived than for the Spaniards to hold the entire world tributary, so that it is not permissible either to buy or to sell except at their good pleasure?[4] In all states we heap odium upon grain speculators and even bring them to punishment; and in very truth there seems to be no other sort of business so disgraceful as that of forcing up prices in the grain market.[5] That is not

[1] Vasquius, same reference.

[2] Vasquius, same reference, n. 5.

[3] In his Works and Days [The entire passage as translated by A. W. Mair (Oxford translation, page 1) is: "For when he that hath no business looketh on him that is rich, he hasteth to plow and to array his house: and neighbour vieth with neighbour hasting to be rich: good is this Strife for men."].

[4] Code IV, 59.

[5] Cajetan on Thomas Aquinas, Summa II. II, q. 77, a. 1, ad 3.

iniuriam, quae in commune fecunda est:[1] neque vero censeri debet in usus paucorum reperta negotiatio, sed ut quod alteri deest alterius copia pensaretur, iusto tamen compendio omnibus proposito, qui laborem ac periculum transferendi in se suscipiunt.

Hoc ipsum igitur quod in republica, id est, minore hominum conventu, grave et perniciosum iudicatur, in magna illa humani generis societate ferendumne est? ut scilicet totius mundi monopolium faciant populi Hispani? Invehitur Ambrosius in eos qui maria claudunt,[2] Augustinus in eos qui itinera obstruunt; Nazianzenus in[3] coemptores suppressoresque mercium, qui ex inopia aliorum soli quaestum faciunt, et ut ipse facundissime loquitur *καταπραγματεύονται τῆς ἐνδείας*. Quin et divini sapientis sententia publicis diris devovetur sacerque habetur, qui alimenta supprimendo vexat annonam: *ὁ συνέχων σῖτον δημοκατάρατος*.

Clament igitur Lusitani quantum, et quam diu libebit: 'Lucra nostra deciditis'. Respondebunt Batavi: 'Immo nostris invigilamus. Hocne indignamini in partem nos venire ventorum et maris? Et quis illa vobis lucra mansura promiserat? Salvum est vobis, quo nos contenti sumus'.

[1] Aristotle, Politica I, 9.
[2] Hexameron V, 10, 4, q. 44.
[3] In funere Basilii.

to be wondered at, for such speculators are doing an injury to nature, who, as Aristotle says, is fertile for all alike.[1] Accordingly it ought not to be supposed that trade was invented for the benefit of a few, but in order that the lack of one would be counterbalanced by the oversupply of another, a fair return also being guaranteed to all who take upon themselves the work and the danger of transport.

Is the same thing then which is considered grievous and pernicious in the smaller community of a state to be put up with at all in that great community of the human race? Shall the people of Spain, forsooth, assume a monopoly of all the world? Ambrose inveighs against those who interfere with the freedom of the sea;[2] Augustine against those who obstruct the overland routes; and Gregory of Nazianzus[3] against those who buy goods and hold them, and thus (as he eloquently says) make profits for themselves alone out of the helplessness and need of others. Indeed in the opinion of this wise and holy man any person who holds back grain and thus forces up the market price ought to be given over to public punishment and be adjudged worthy of death.

Therefore the Portuguese may cry as loud and as long as they shall please: 'You are cutting down our profits'! The Dutch will answer: 'Nay! we are but looking out for our own interests! Are you angry because we share with you in the winds and the sea? Pray, who had promised that you would always have those advantages? You are secure in the possession of that with which we are quite content'.

[1] Politics I, 9.
[2] Hexameron V, 10, 4, q. 44.
[3] In funere Basilii.

CAPVT XIII

Batavis ius commercii Indicani qua pace, qua indutiis, qua bello retinendum

Quare cum et ius et aequum postulet, libera nobis ita ut cuiquam esse Indiae commercia, superest, ut sive cum Hispanis pax, sive indutiae fiunt, sive bellum manet, omnino eam, quam a natura habemus libertatem tueamur. Nam ad pacem quod attinet, notum est eam esse duorum generum: aut enim pari foedere, aut impari coitur. Graeci[1] istam vocant *συνθήκην ἐξ ἴσου* hanc *σπονδὰς ἐξ ἐπιταγμάτων* illa virorum est, haec ingeniorum servilium. Demosthenes in oratione de libertate Rhodiorum:[2] *καί τοι χρὴ τοὺς βουλομένους ἐλευθέρους εἶναι τὰς ἐκ τῶν ἐπιταγμάτων συνθήκας φεύγειν, ὡς ἐγγὺς δουλείας οὔσας,* 'eos qui volunt esse liberi oportet omnes condiciones quibus leges imponuntur ita fugere tamquam quae proximae sunt servituti'. Tales autem sunt omnes quibus pars altera in iure suo imminuitur, iuxta Isocratis definitionem[3] vocantis *τὰ τοὺς ἑτέρους ἐλαττοῦντα παρὰ τὸ δίκαιον.* Si enim, ut inquit Cicero,[4] 'suscipienda bella sunt ob eam causam, ut sine iniuria in pace vivatur', sequitur eodem auctore *, pacem esse vocandam, non pactionem servitutis, sed tranquillam libertatem; quippe cum et Philosophorum et Theologorum

[1] Thucydides, Isocrates, Andocides.
[2] Isocrates, Archidamos 51.
[3] Panegyricus 176.
[4] De officiis I, 35.
* [Philippica XII, 14: cum iis facta pax non erit pax, sed pactio servitutis.]

CHAPTER XIII

The Dutch must maintain their right of trade with the East Indies by peace, by treaty, or by war

Wherefore since both law and equity demand that trade with the East Indies be as free to us as to any one else, it follows that we are to maintain at all hazards that freedom which is ours by nature, either by coming to a peace agreement with the Spaniards, or by concluding a treaty, or by continuing the war. So far as peace is concerned, it is well known that there are two kinds of peace, one made on terms of equality, the other on unequal terms. The Greeks [1] call the former kind a compact between equals, the latter an enjoined truce; the former is meant for high souled men, the latter for servile spirits. Demosthenes in his speech on the liberty of the Rhodians [2] says that it was necessary for those who wished to be free to keep away from treaties which were imposed upon them, because such treaties were almost the same as slavery. Such conditions are all those by which one party is lessened in its own right, according to the definition of Isocrates.[3] For if, as Cicero says,[4] wars must be undertaken in order that people may live in peace unharmed, it follows that peace ought to mean not an agreement which entails slavery, but an undisturbed liberty, especially as peace and justice according to

[1] Thucydides, Isocrates, Andocides.
[2] Isocrates, Archidamos 51 [Grotius probably quoted here from memory].
[3] Panegyric 176.
[4] De officiis I, 35.

complurium[1] iudicio pax et iustitia nominibus magis quam re differant, sitque pax non qualiscumque, sed ordinata concordia.

Indutiae autem si fiunt satis apparet ex ipsa indutiarum natura non debere medio earum tempore condicionem cuiusquam deteriorem fieri, cum ferme interdicti uti possidetis instar obtineant.

Quod si in bellum trudimur hostium iniquitate, debet nobis causae aequitas spem ac fiduciam boni eventus addere. Nam[2] *ὑπὲρ ὧν ἂν ἐλαττῶνται μεχρὶ δυνατοῦ πάντες πολεμοῦσι, περὶ δὲ τοῦ πλεονεκτεῖν οὐχ οὕτως,* 'pro his in quibus iniuria afficiuntur omnes quantum omnino possunt depugnant: at propter alieni cupiditatem non item'; quod et Alexander Imperator ita expressit: *τὸ μὲν ἄρχειν ἀδίκων ἔργων οὐκ ἀγνώμονα ἔχει τὴν πρόκλησιν, τὸ δὲ τοὺς ὀχλοῦντας ἀποσείεσθαι ἔκ τε τῆς ἀγαθῆς συνειδήσεως ἔχει τὸ θαῤῥαλέον, καὶ ἐκ τοῦ μὴ ἀδικεῖν ἀλλ' ἀμύνασθαι ὑπάρχει τὸ εὔελπι,* 'eius a quo coepit iniuria, provocatio maxime invidiosa est; at cum depelluntur aggressores, sicut bona conscientia fiduciam secum fert, ita quia de vindicanda non de inferenda iniuria laboratur, spes etiam adsunt optimae'.

Si ita necesse est, perge gens mari invictissima, nec tuam tantum, sed humani generis libertatem audacter propugna.

Nec te, quod classis centenis remigat alis,
Terreat: INVITO labitur illa MARI:
Quodve vehunt prorae Centaurica saxa minantes,
Tigna cava et pictos experiere metus.
Frangit et attollit vires in milite causa;
Quae nisi iusta subest, excutit arma pudor.[3]

[1] Polus Lucanus apud Stobaeum, De iustitia (III, p. 362 Wachsmut-Hense); Clemens Alexandrinus, Stromateis; Augustinus, De civitate Dei IV, 15.

[2] Demosthenes, De libertate Rhodiorum XV, 10 (p. 193 R.).

[3] Propertius IV, vi, 47-52.

the opinion of many philosophers and theologians [1] differ more in name than in fact, and as peace is a harmonious agreement based not on individual whim, but on well ordered regulations.

If however a truce is arranged for, it is quite clear from the very nature of a truce, that during its continuance no one's condition ought to change for the worse, inasmuch as both parties stand on the equivalent of a *uti possidetis.*

But if we are driven into war by the injustice of our enemies, the justice of our cause ought to bring hope and confidence in a happy outcome. "For," as Demosthenes has said, "every one fights his hardest to recover what he has lost; but when men endeavor to gain at the expense of others it is not so." [2] The Emperor Alexander has expressed his idea in this way: 'Those who begin unjust deeds, must bear the greatest blame; but those who repel aggressors are twice armed, both with courage because of their just cause, and with the highest hope because they are not doing a wrong, but are warding off a wrong'.

Therefore, if it be necessary, arise, O nation unconquered on the sea, and fight boldly, not only for your own liberty, but for that of the human race. "Nor let it fright thee that their fleet is winged, each ship, with an hundred oars. The sea whereon it sails will have none of it. And though the prows bear figures threatening to cast rocks such as Centaurs throw, thou shalt find them but hollow planks and painted terrors. 'Tis his cause that makes or mars a soldier's strength. If the cause be not just, shame strikes the weapon from his hands." [3]

[1] Polus Lucanus apud Stobaeum, De iustitia; Clemens Alexandrinus, Strumateis; Augustine, City of God IV, 15.

[2] On the liberty of the Rhodians XV, 10 [Pickard-Cambridge's translation I, page 59].

[3] Propertius IV, vi, 47-52 [Butler's (Loeb) translation, page 305].

Si iusta multi, et ipse Augustinus,[1] arma crediderunt eo nomine suscipi, quod per terras alienas iter innoxium negaretur, quanto illa erunt iustiora, quibus maris, quod naturae lege commune est, usus communis et innoxius postulatur? Si iuste oppugnatae sunt gentes quae in suo solo commercia aliis interdicebant, quid illae quae populos ad se nihil pertinentes per vim distinent, ac mutuos earum commeatus intercludunt? Si res ista in iudicio agitaretur, dubitari non potest quae a viro bono expectari deberet sententia, ait Praetor:[2] 'Quo minus illi in flumine publico navem agere, ratem agere, quove minus per ripam exonerare liceat, vim fieri veto'. De mari et litore in eandem formam dandum interdictum docent interpretes, exemplo Labeonis, qui cum interdiceret Praetor:[3] 'Ne quid in flumine publico ripave eius facias, quo statio iterve navigio deterius sit, fiat'; simile dixit interdictum competere in mari:[4] 'Ne quid in mari inve litore facias, quo portus, statio, iterve navigio deterius sit, fiat'.

Immo et post prohibitionem, si quis scilicet in mari navigare prohibitus sit, aut non permissus rem suam vendere, aut re sua uti, iniuriarum eo nomine competere actionem Vlpianus respondit.[5] Theologi insuper et qui tractant casus, quos vocant, conscientiarum, concordes tra-

[1] De civitate Dei V, 1.

[2] Digest XLIII, 14, 1 (Ut in flumine publico navigare liceat).

[3] Digest XLIII, 12, 1 (De fluminibus, L. 1, in principio).

[4] Digest XLIII, 12, 1 (De fluminibus, L. 1, § Si in mari aliquid).

[5] Digest XLIII, 8, 2 (Ne quid in loco publico, L. 2, § Si quis); XLVII, 10, 13 et 24 (De iniuriis, L. Iniuriarum actio, et L. Si quis proprium); Silvestris, In verbo 'restitutio', 3 sub finem; Oldradus et Archidiaconus on Digest XLVIII, 12, 2 (De lege Iulia de annona), and XLVII, 11, 6 (De extraordinariis criminibus. L. Annonam).

If many writers, Augustine himself[1] among them, believed it was right to take up arms because innocent passage was refused across foreign territory, how much more justly will arms be taken up against those from whom the demand is made of the common and innocent use of the sea, which by the law of nature is common to all? If those nations which interdicted others from trade on their own soil are justly attacked, what of those nations which separate by force and interrupt the mutual intercourse of peoples over whom they have no rights at all? If this case should be taken into court, there can be no doubt what opinion ought to be anticipated from a just judge. The praetor's law says:[2] ' I forbid force to be used in preventing any one from sailing a ship or a boat on a public river, or from unloading his cargo on the bank '. The commentators say that the injunction must be applied in the same manner to the sea and to the seashore. Labeo, for example, in commenting on the praetor's edict,[3] ' Let nothing be done in a public river or on its bank, by which a landing or a channel for shipping be obstructed ', said there was a similar interdict which applied to the sea, namely,[4] ' Let nothing be done on the sea or on the seashore by which a harbor, a landing, or a channel for shipping be obstructed '.

Nay more, after such a prohibition, if, namely, a man be prevented from navigating the sea, or not allowed to sell or to make use of his own wares and products, Ulpian says that he can bring an action for damages on that ground.[5] Also the theologians and the casuists agree that he who prevents another from buying or selling, or who puts his

[1] City of God V, 1.

[2] Digest XLIII, 14, 1.

[3] Digest XLIII, 12, 1.

[4] Digest XLIII, 12, 1.

[5] Digest XLIII, 8, 2; XLVII, 10, 13 and 24; Silvestris, on the word ' restitutio '; Oldradus and Archidiaconus on Digest XLVIII, 12, 2, and XLVII, 11, 6 [Oldrado de Ponte (?-1335), a Bologna canonist. Archidiaconus is probably the Italian decretalist Guido Bosius.]

dunt, eum qui alterum vendere aut emere impediat, utilitatemve propriam publicae ac communi praeponat, aut ullo modo alterum in eo quod est iuris communis impediat, ad restitutionem teneri omnis damni viri boni arbitrio.

Secundum haec igitur vir bonus iudicans, Batavis libertatem commerciorum adiudicaret, Lusitanos et ceteros, qui eam libertatem impediunt, vetaret vim facere, et damna restituere iuberet. Quod autem in iudicio obtineretur, id ubi iudicium haberi non potest, iusto bello vindicatur. Augustinus:[1] 'Iniquitas partis adversae iusta ingerit bella'. Et Cicero:[2] 'Cum sint duo genera decertandi, unum per disceptationem, alterum per vim, confugiendum ad posterius, si uti non licet priore'. Et Rex Theodoricus: 'Veniendum tunc ad arma, cum locum apud adversarium iustitia non potest reperire'. Et quod proprius est nostro argumento,[3] Pomponius eum qui rem omnibus communem cum incommodo ceterorum usurpet, MANV PROHIBENDVM respondit. Theologi quoque tradunt, sicuti pro rerum cuiusque defensione bellum recte suscipitur, ita non minus recte suscipi, pro usu earum rerum quae naturali iure debent esse communes. Quare ei qui itinera praecludat, evectionemque mercium impediat, etiam non expectata ulla publica auctoritate, *via facti,* ut loquuntur, posse occurri.

Quae cum ita sint, minime verendum est, ne aut Deus

[1] De civitate Dei IV.

[2] De officiis I, 34.

[3] Digest XLI, 1, 50 (De adquirendo rerum dominio, L. Quamvis quod in litore); Henricus von Gorcum, De bello justo 9.

private interests before the public and common interests, or who in any way hinders another in the use of something which is his by common right, is held in damages to complete restitution in an amount fixed by an honorable arbitrator.

Following these principles a good judge would award to the Dutch the freedom of trade, and would forbid the Portuguese and others from using force to hinder that freedom, and would order the payment of just damages. But when a judgment which would be rendered in a court cannot be obtained, it should with justice be demanded in a war. Augustine[1] acknowledges this when he says: 'The injustice of an adversary brings a just war'. Cicero also says:[2] "There are two ways of settling a dispute; first, by discussion; second, by physical force; we must resort to force only in case we may not avail ourselves of discussion." And King Theodoric says: 'Recourse must then be had to arms when justice can find no lodgment in an adversary's heart'. Pomponius, however, has handed down a decision which has more bearing on our argument[3] than any of the citations already made. He declared that the man who seized a thing common to all to the prejudice of every one else must be forcibly prevented from so doing. The theologians also say that just as war is righteously undertaken in defense of individual property, so no less righteously is it undertaken in behalf of the use of those things which by natural law ought to be common property. Therefore he who closes up roads and hinders the export of merchandise ought to be prevented from so doing *via facti,* even without waiting for any public authority.

Since these things are so, there need not be the slightest

[1] City of God IV.
[2] De officiis I, 34 [Walter Miller's (Loeb) translation, page 37].
[3] Digest XLI, 1, 50; Heinrich von Gorcum, De bello justo 9.

eorum conatus secundet, qui ab ipso institutum ius naturae certissimum violant, aut homines ipsi eos inultos patiantur, qui solo quaestus sui respectu communem humani generis utilitatem oppugnant.

fear that God will prosper the efforts of those who violate that most stable law of nature which He himself has instituted, or that even men will allow those to go unpunished who for the sake alone of private gain oppose a common benefit of the human race.

CVM SVB HOC TEMPVS PLVRIMAE REGIS HISPANIARVM LITTERAE IN MANVS NOSTRAS VENISSENT, QVIBVS IPSIVS ET LVSITANORVM INSTITVTVM MANIFESTE DETEGITVR, OPERAE PRETIVM VISVM EST EX IIS, QVAE PLERAEQVE EODEM ERANT ARGVMENTO, BINAS IN LATINVM SERMONEM TRANSLATAS EXHIBERE.

Domine Martine Alphonse de Castro, Prorex amice, ego Rex multam tibi salutem mitto:

Cum hisce litteris perveniet ad te exemplum typis impressum Edicti quod faciendum curavi, quo, ob rationes quas expressas videbis, aliasque meis rebus conducentes prohibeo commercium omne externorum in ipsis partibus Indiae aliisque regionibus transmarinis. Quandoquidem res haec est momenti atque usus maximi, et quae effici summa cum industria debeat, impero tibi, ut simulatque litteras has et edictum acceperis, publicationem eius omni diligentia procures in omnibus locis ac partibus istius imperi, idque ipsum quod edicto continetur exsequaris sine ullius personae exceptione, cuiuscumque qualitatis, aetatis, condicionisve sit, citra omnem moram atque excusationem, procedasque ad impletionem mandati via merae exsecutionis, nullo admisso impedimento, appellatione, aut gravamine in contrarium, cuiuscumque materiae generis aut qualitatis. Iubeo itaque hoc ipsum impleri per eos ministros ad quos exsecutio pertinet, iisque significari, non modo eos qui contra fecerint malam operam mihi navaturos, sed eosdem me puniturum privatione officiorum in quibus mihi serviunt.

Quia autem relatum est mihi commorari in istis partibus

APPENDIX

Two letters of Philip III, King of Spain

As several letters of the King of Spain have come of late into our hands, in which his design and that of the Portuguese is clearly disclosed, it seemed worth while to translate into Latin two of them which had particular bearing upon the controversy at issue, and to append them here.

LETTER I

To Don Martin Alfonso de Castro, our beloved viceroy, I, the King, send many greetings:

Together with this letter will come to you a copy printed in type of an edict which I have taken much pains to draw up, by which, for reasons which you will see expressed, and for other reasons which are consonant with my interests, I prohibit all commerce of foreigners in India itself, and in all other regions across the seas. As this matter is of the greatest importance and serviceableness, and ought to be carried out with the highest zeal, I command you, as soon as you shall have received this letter and edict, to further with all diligence its publication in all places and districts under your jurisdiction, and to carry out the provisions of the edict without exception of any person whatsoever, no matter what his quality, age, or condition, and without delay and excuse, and to proceed to the fulfilment of this command with the full power of your authority, no delay, appeal, or obstacle to the contrary, being admitted, of any kind, sort, or quality.

Therefore I order that this duty be discharged by those

externos multos variarum nationum, Italos, Gallos, Germanos, Belgas, quorum pars maior, quantum intelligimus, eo venit per Persida et Turcarum imperium, non per hoc regnum, adversus quos si ex huius Edicti praescripto ac rigore procedatur, posse inde nonnullas difficultates sequi, si illi ad Mauros inimicos perfugiant, vicinisque munitionum mearum dispositionem indicent, rationesque monstrent quae rebus meis nocere possent, exsequi te hoc edictum volo prout res et tempus ferent, atque ea uti prudentia, qua illae difficultates evitentur, curando ut omnes externos in potestate tua habeas eosque custodias pro cuiusque qualitate, ita ut adversus imperium nostrum nihil valeant attentare, utque ergo omnino eum finem consequar quem hoc Edicto mihi proposui.

Scriptae Vlyssipone XXVIII Novembris, Anno MDCVI. Subsignatum erat Rex. Inscriptio. Pro Rege. Ad Dominum Martinum Alfonsum de Castro Consiliarium suum, et suum Proregem Indiae.

Prorex amice Rex multam salutem tibi mitto:

Etsi pro certo habeo tua praesentia, iisque viribus cum quibus in partes austrinas concessisti, perduelles Hollandos,

officers to whom its execution belongs, and that they be informed that not only will those who disobey serve me ill, but that I will punish them by depriving them of the offices in which they now serve me.

Further, inasmuch as it has been reported to me that within your jurisdiction there are sojourning many foreigners of different nations, Italians, French, Germans, and men of the Low Countries, the larger part of whom as we know came there by way of Persia and Turkey, and not through our realm; and inasmuch as, if this edict be rigidly enforced against those persons to the letter, some inconveniences might follow, if they should escape to the Moors, our enemies, and make known to our neighbors the disposition of my forces, and thus show ways that they might be able to harm my dominion: Therefore, I wish you to carry out the provisions of this edict as the exigencies of circumstances and occasion demand, and to use all prudence necessary in order to avoid those difficulties, taking especial pains to keep all foreigners in your power, and to guard them in accordance with their individual rank, so that they may have no opportunity to attempt anything prejudicial to our power, that thus I may attain fully that end which I have set forth in this edict.

Given at Lisbon, on the 28th of November in the year of our Lord, 1606. Signed by the king, and addressed: For the king, to Don Martin Alfonso de Castro, his Councillor, and Viceroy for the East Indies.

LETTER II

To our beloved viceroy, I, the King send many greetings:

Although I consider it absolutely certain that your presence and the forces which you took with you into those Eastern regions, guarantee that our enemies, the Dutch,

qui illic haerent, nec minus indigenas qui eis receptum praebent, ita castigatos fore, ut nec hi, nec illi tale quicquam in posterum audeant; expediet tamen, ad res tuendas, ut iustam classem, eique operi idoneam, cum tu Goam redibis, in istis Maris partibus relinquas, eiusque imperium et summam praefecturam mandes Andreae Hurtado Mendosae, aut si quem ei muneri aptiorem iudicabis, quemadmodum pro tuo in me affectu confido, ea in re non aliud te respecturum quam quod rebus meis erit utilissimum.

Scriptae Madritii XXVII Ian. MDCVII. Signatum Rex. Inscriptio. Pro Rege. Ad Dominum Martinum Alfonsum de Castro suum Consiliarium, et suum Proregem Indiae.

who infest those quarters as well as the natives who give them a welcome reception, will be so thoroughly punished that neither the one nor the other will ever dare such practices in the future: still it will be expedient for the protection of our interests, that, when you shall return to Goa, you leave in those parts of the sea a fleet large and capable enough to do the business, and also that you delegate the supreme command of that fleet to Andrea Hurtado de Mendoza, or to any one else whom you shall consider better fitted for this post. I rely upon your affection for me, knowing that in this matter you will do nothing but what will be most useful to my interests.

Given at Madrid the 27th day of January in the year of our Lord 1607. Signed by the king, and addressed: For the king, to Don Martin Alfonso de Castro, his Councillor, and Viceroy for the East Indies.

INDEX

References are to pages of text and translation alike.

THE EVOLUTION OF CAPITALISM

Allen, Zachariah. **The Practical Tourist,** Or Sketches of the State of the Useful Arts, and of Society, Scenery, &c. &c. in Great-Britain, France and Holland. Providence, R.I., 1832. Two volumes in one.

Bridge, James Howard. **The Inside History of the Carnegie Steel Company:** A Romance of Millions. New York, 1903.

Brodrick, J[ames]. **The Economic Morals of the Jesuits:** An Answer to Dr. H. M. Robertson. London, 1934.

Burlamaqui, J[ean-] J[acques]. **The Principles of Natural and Politic Law.** Cambridge, Mass., 1807. Two volumes in one.

Capitalism and Fascism: Three Right-Wing Tracts, 1937-1941. New York, 1972.

Corey, Lewis. **The Decline of American Capitalism.** New York, 1934.

[Court, Pieter de la]. **The True Interest and Political Maxims, of the Republic of Holland.** Written by that Great Statesman and Patriot, John de Witt. To which is prefixed, (never before printed) Historical Memoirs of the Illustrious Brothers Cornelius and John de Witt, by John Campbell. London, 1746.

Dos Passos, John R. **Commercial Trusts:** The Growth and Rights of Aggregated Capital. An Argument Delivered Before the Industrial Commission at Washington, D.C., December 12, 1899. New York, 1901.

Fanfani, Amintore. **Catholicism, Protestantism and Capitalism.** London, 1935.

Gaskell, P[eter]. **The Manufacturing Population of England:** Its Moral, Social, and Physical Conditions, and the Changes Which Have Arisen From the Use of Steam Machinery; With an Examination of Infant Labour. London, 1833.

Göhre, Paul. **Three Months in a Workshop:** A Practical Study. London, 1895.

Greeley, Horace. **Essays Designed to Elucidate the Science of Political Economy,** While Serving to Explain and Defend the Policy of Protection to Home Industry, As a System of National Cooperation for the Elevation of Labor. Boston, 1870.

Grotius, Hugo. **The Freedom of the Seas,** Or, The Right Which Belongs to the Dutch to Take Part in the East Indian Trade. Translated with Revision of the Latin Text of 1633 by Ralph Van Deman Magoffin. New York, 1916.

Hadley, Arthur Twining. **Economics:** An Account of the Relations Between Private Property and Public Welfare. New York, 1896.

Knight, Charles. **Capital and Labour;** Including *The Results of Machinery.* London, 1845.

de Malynes, Gerrard. **Englands View, in the Unmasking of Two Paradoxes:** With a Replication unto the Answer of Maister John Bodine. London, 1603. New Introduction by Mark Silk.

Marquand, H. A. **The Dynamics of Industrial Combination.** London, 1931.

Mercantilist Views of Trade and Monopoly: Four Essays, 1645-1720. New York, 1972.

Morrison, C[harles]. **An Essay on the Relations Between Labour and Capital.** London, 1854.

Nicholson, J. Shield. **The Effects of Machinery on Wages.** London, 1892.

One Hundred Years' Progress of the United States: With an Appendix Entitled Marvels That Our Grandchildren Will See; or, One Hundred Years' Progress in the Future. By Eminent Literary Men, Who Have Made the Subjects on Which They Have Written Their Special Study. Hartford, Conn., 1870.

The Poetry of Industry: Two Literary Reactions to the Industrial Revolution, 1755/1757. New York, 1972.

Pre-Capitalist Economic Thought: Three Modern Interpretations. New York, 1972.

Promoting Prosperity: Two Eighteenth Century Tracts. New York, 1972.

Proudhon, P[ierre-] J[oseph]. **System of Economical Contradictions:** Or, The Philosophy of Misery. (Reprinted from *The Works of P. J. Proudhon,* Vol. IV, Part I.) Translated by Benj. R. Tucker. Boston, 1888.

Religious Attitudes Toward Usury: Two Early Polemics. New York, 1972.

Roscher, William. **Principles of Political Economy.** New York, 1878. Two volumes in one.

Scoville, Warren C. **Revolution in Glassmaking:** Entrepreneurship and Technological Change in the American Industry, 1880-1920. Cambridge, Mass., 1948.

Selden, John. **Of the Dominion, Or, Ownership of the Sea.** Written at First in Latin, and Entituled *Mare Clausum.* Translated by Marchamont Nedham. London, 1652.

Senior, Nassau W. **Industrial Efficiency and Social Economy.** Original Manuscript Arranged and Edited by S. Leon Levy. New York, 1928. Revised Preface by S. Leon Levy. Two volumes in one.

Spann, Othmar. **The History of Economics.** Translated from the 19th German Edition by Eden and Cedar Paul. New York, 1930.

The Usury Debate After Adam Smith: Two Nineteenth Century Essays. New York, 1972. New Introduction by Mark Silk.

The Usury Debate in the Seventeenth Century: Three Arguments. New York, 1972.

Varga, E[ugen]. **Twentieth Century Capitalism.** Translated from the Russian by George H. Hanna. Moscow, [1964].

Young, Arthur. **Arthur Young on Industry and Economics**: Being Excerpts from Arthur Young's Observations on the State of Manufactures and His Economic Opinions on Problems Related to Contemporary Industry in England. Arranged by Elizabeth Pinney Hunt. Bryn Mawr, Pa., 1926.

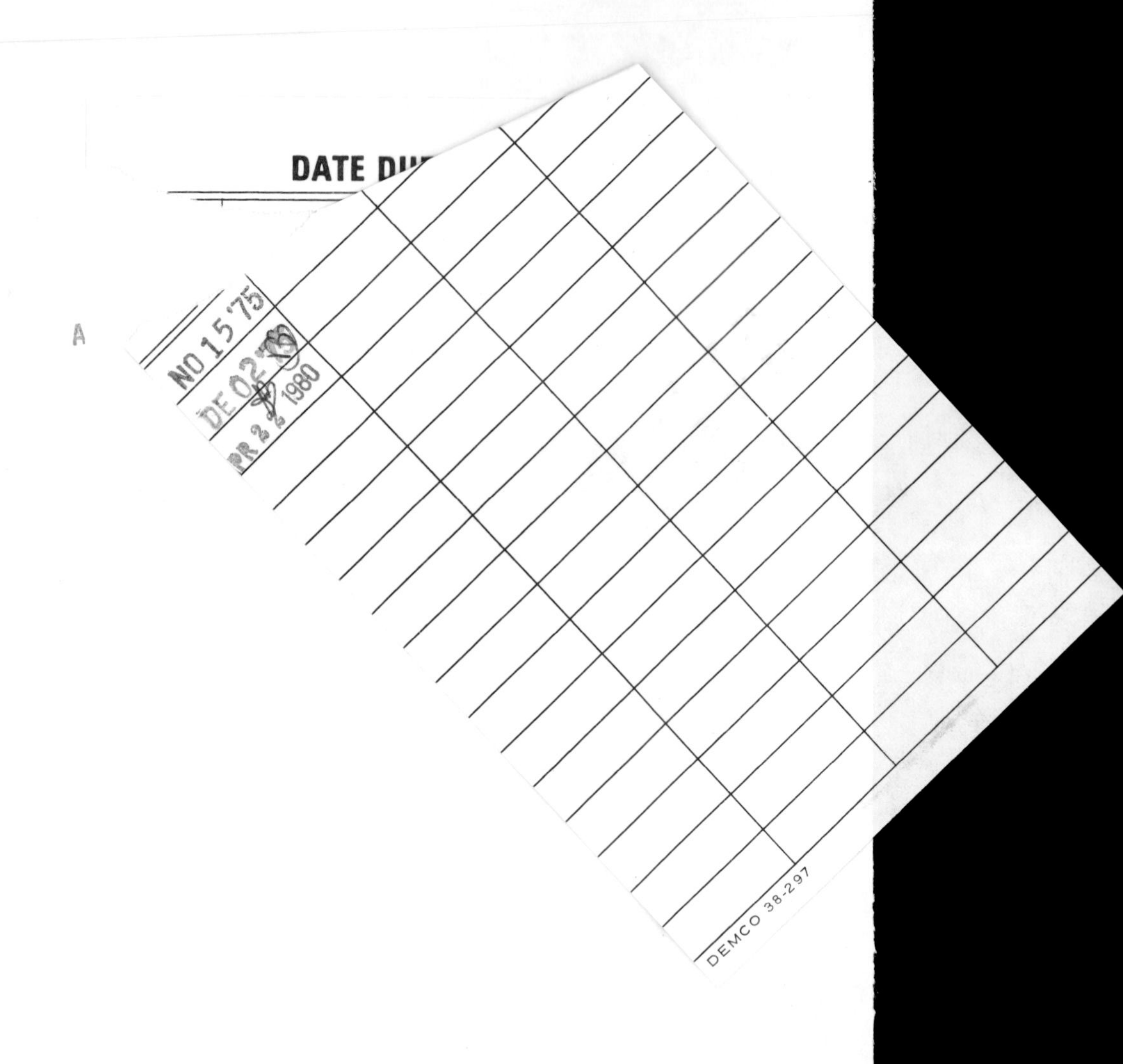
DATE DU
NO 15 '75
DE 02 '
PR 2 1980
DEMCO 38-297